The Essential Bu

C000146052

VOLKSWAGEN
GOLF GTI

Your marque experts: Ken Cservenka & Richard Copping

VELOCE PUBLISHING
THE PUBLISHER OF FINE AUTOMOTIVE BOOKS

Also from Veloce Publishing

www.veloce.co.uk

First published in February 2009 by Veloce Publishing Limited, 33 Trinity Street, Dorchester DT1 1TT, England. Fax 01305 268864/e-mail info@veloce.co.uk/web www.veloce.co.uk or www.velocebooks.com. ISBN: 978-1-84584-188-1 UPC: 636847041885

Introduction
– the purpose of this book

By purchasing this book you must be contemplating buying a classic Volkswagen Golf. Our intention is to concentrate on the iconic Mk1 and the increasingly collectable, but eminently affordable, Mk2 in GTI or linked guise. Some might be seeking out a Cabriolet version as a weekend fun car, and if this is the case, you're in luck, because we've covered this option too.

This early Mk1 GTI can be identified by the girder-style bumpers. White wheels, etc, are non-standard.

Should you decide to attend Britain's biggest annual gathering of the hot hatch fraternity, GTI International, you might have difficulty finding many Mk1 or Mk2 GTIs that haven't received what most would describe as 'the treatment'. Spectacularly wide alloys abound, lowered and stiffened suspension is evident in profusion, the number of meaty and throaty exhausts is second only to the chipped, boosted, and generally upgraded engines. Within the confines of this book it is impossible for us to describe and analyse every upgrade, but it is practical for us to consider general themes along such lines. And for those whose intention it is to purchase a car that appears today as it did when it left Wolfsburg, we've certainly got that angle comprehensively covered. For would-be restorers, we indicate the Golf's weakest points, and the costliest, most difficult, parts to obtain.

The 16-valve Mk2 GTI is a sought-after hot hatch and, when finished in Tornado Red, really looks the part.

As enthusiasts of the Golf ourselves – we've written about them and photographed them for many a year, culminating in the *Veloce* volume entitled 'VW Golf - Five Generations of Fun' – we feel that we're at least one step ahead of the crowd. Show us a Rallye Golf, quiz us about eight- and sixteen-valve preferences, query us about originality, and you should have an answer somewhere in this book.

Most hot Mk1 and Mk2 Golfs aren't going to break the bank when purchased. Our primary purpose is to assist you in making sure that your acquisition isn't going to cost you a fortune in the future through your lack of experience when parting with your hard-earned cash.

Ken Cservenka & Richard Copping

The Rallye Golf is a powerful beast and also in demand. However, if things go wrong, it can be costly to repair!

Contents

1 Is it the right car for you?
– marriage guidance

Tall and short drivers
Comparable to a modern day Volkswagen Polo, both the Mk1 and Mk2 Golf GTI are eminently suited to all shapes and sizes of driver!

Weight of controls
With 239mm ventilated discs up front but only 180x30mm drums at the rear the Mk1 GTI came in for some criticism, happily remedied on the Mk2 GTI, which was equipped with 226mm solid discs on the rear wheels. The lack of power-steering in both generations (fortunately optional on Mk2 GTIs and standard from 1990) will come as a shock to the system!

Will it fit in the garage?
With an overall length of around 3985mm, dependent on which style of bumper is fitted, and a width of 1680mm, the larger Mk2 will fit into even the smallest of garages.

Interior space
Think modern VW Polo and you have the comfort of a genuine four- or five-seat car.

Luggage capacity
For the Mk1: 13cu.ft with the rear seat up and 35.7cu.ft with it down; Mk2: 14.4cu.ft and 50.3cu.ft, respectively.

Running costs
Let's be honest, no GTI has ever been particularly frugal with fuel. Most spares can be found at reasonable prices, although the official dealer network guys might look blank – or rub their hands with glee.

Usability
Few people buy a GTI for purposes other than to use – after all the Mk1 is the original hot hatch. As for the Mk2, specifically in 16-valve guise, you're looking at 130mph and 0-60 in 7.9 seconds where the law permits.

Parts availability
Mk1 restorers complain that complete originality is bordering on impossible, but for many there are ways and means to overcome hard-to-come-by cosmetic items. The Mk2 currently poses few, if any, problems.

Parts cost
With a reasonably large aftermarket presence, prices aren't that bad. Tweak the standard specification and great goodies often come with hefty price tags.

Insurance group
Keep it standard, accept a restricted mileage, and classic car insurance is an option. Go circuit racing, or cram additional beefy power in the engine bay, and costs escalate.

Investment potential
No Mk1 GTI is going to cost a fortune ... yet. Some Mk2 examples, admittedly in need of a little TLC, are readily available at pocket-money prices. Give it a few years though, and we confidently predict that prices will be going up.

Foibles
Not that many really – early GTIs were only available in left-hand-drive form, as was the Rallye Golf. A further extra hot Mk2, the G60, wasn't produced for the British market, so that too is a left hooker.

Plus points
Both the Mk1 and Mk2 look good in GTI guise, while it won't cost a fortune to add a personal touch if that's desired. Mk2 models were thoroughly coated with protective wax; all are great fun to drive with excellent performance.

Minus points
The dated appearance of the Mk1's interior might raise the odd eyebrow, and rust was certainly a menace as far as the early pre '80 model year GTIs went. The lack of power-steering on all Mk1 cars and its absence as standard for most of the production run of the Mk2 makes many first and second generation GTIs heavy to manoeuvre. Think superchargers and a limited durability – Rallye Golf and the G60.

Alternatives
As Volkswagen enthusiasts through and through, the only options we might suggest would be either the Mk1 or Mk2 Scirocco, or the rather tasty and genuinely powerful Corrado.

Comfortable, but a firmer ride than a family saloon.

2 Cost considerations
– affordable, or a money pit?

The manufacturer recommends a service interval of every 10,000 miles or 15,000km, or once a year minimum for most lubrication and adjustment cycles, with a change of cam-belt at every 40,000 miles or 60,000km. Brake fluid should be changed every two years.

Small service: ● x80 from independent VW specialist
Large service: ● x160 from independent VW specialist
New clutch: (not fitted) ● x80 (fitted) ● x200
Rebuilt engine, no ancillaries: (not fitted) 1600cc or 1800cc 8v ● x1500, 1800cc 16v ● x1600
Rebuilt engine: (fitted with all ancillaries attached, ready to drive away) 1600cc or 1800cc 8v ● x2500, 1800cc 16v ● x2600
Rebuilt gearbox: (not fitted) ● x400
8v cylinder head (each, not fitted): from ● x360
16v cylinder head (each, not fitted): from ● x490
Rebuilt supercharger: G60 and Rallye Golf: from (not fitted) ● x355 (fitted and reset on the car) from ● x450. Pulley kit giving 30bhp extra power from ● x195
Change cam-belt: from ● x145
Front disc: ● x25
Brake drum: rear Mk1 ● x25
Brake disc: rear Mk2 ● x25
Brake pads: from ● x19, Mk2 rear ● x16
Brake shoes: rear Mk1 ● x16
Brake callipers: front ● x80, Mk2 rear ● x65
Brake servo: Mk1 ● x150
Steering rack: ● x60
Suspension kits, often including lowered springs and up-rated dampers: from ● x250
Strut inserts: from Mk1 ● x40, Mk2 ● x32, rear Mk1 and Mk2 ● x35
New headlight: Genuine Hella or Bosch ● x40
Exhaust system (not fitted) Mk1: ● x110
Exhaust down pipe Mk1: ● x38
Exhaust system (not fitted) Mk2 8v: ● x140
Exhaust down pipe Mk2 8v: ● x50
Exhaust system (not fitted) Mk2 16v: ● x240
Exhaust down pipe Mk2 16v: ● x68
Mk2 bumper: from ● x55
Full re-spray (inc preparation): from ● x2000
Full professional restoration of a GTI in poor condition: from ● x4000

A black girder bumper with plastic end caps, a feature of the earliest GTIs – could be difficult to find and expensive to replace.

Parts that are easy to find: Service items and engine parts
Parts that are hard to find: Original VW body panels, trim and seals for interior and exterior, especially for Mk1
Parts that are very expensive: Most special equipment for G60 and Rallye Golf. Digifant ECU. Digifant control unit repaired from ● x250, new – don't ask!

3 Living with a Mk1 or Mk2 Golf
– will you get along together?

It is entirely realistic to suggest that a well maintained Mk1 or Mk2 GTI could be used as fast and furious daily transport. The same would be true of the less well-known models we have chosen to brand as specials – the Rallye Golf and the G60.

If these cars are perfectly capable of keeping pace with 21st century motoring, it's equally appropriate to declare them ideal as a second vehicle to be used as a practical classic at weekends and on holidays. While some owners delight in entering their pride and joy in the ever-growing number of Volkswagen Concours events held across the country, and others might be content to enjoy their GTI to the full on some of the open roads in less heavily populated areas, many trek miles to take part in quarter-mile sprints and fast track-day activities. Whether GTIs given extra breath to star in such events can legitimately be called practical classics is a matter of personal opinion. What we do know is that the beefed-up Mk1 or Mk2 GTI has a big, big following.

A reasonable number of owners are keen to participate in the rewarding Concours merry-go-round.

A popular pastime for many GTI owners is to attend a track day event, to give the car a thrashing not possible on public roads.

As for the apparently genteel Cabriolet – as with all soft-top models – it's more vulnerable to vandalism, while watertight accommodation with an elderly hood might not always be achievable. Mechanically, it's a Golf and that's the end of the matter. Structurally, of course, the Cabriolet is less rigid than the hatch, while an extra cross member, deeper sills and other strengthening measures add a speed-deadening 100kg to the car's weight. Conversely, if Mk1 styling is your preference, the Cabriolet stayed in production for 13 years as a Mk2 version was never offered. Its replacement didn't appear until 1994 at a point when the Mk3 hatch had already been in production for a couple of years.

In our opinion, once you have joined the Mk1 or Mk2 fraternity you won't look back. Having more-or-less exterminated the rusting problems that blighted the earliest of Golfs – more of which elsewhere – Volkswagen could luxuriate in the reputation for reliability and longevity it had first acquired in the days of the old air-cooled models. You will benefit from these undoubted strengths of the marque and – for complete reassurance – compare surviving examples produced by other manufacturers. Need we say more?

It's more important to buy a Cabrio with a hood in good condition than to demand a black hood for originality's sake.

This discreet little hook on the engine cover hinge is only found on the Rallye Golf, and is designed to prevent the bonnet flying open during motorsport events.

4 Relative values
– which model for you?

Golf GTI and associated model lineage is relatively straightforward but, we'll take time and care to list each model here as, in just a couple of cases, you need to be aware of the potential pitfalls of ownership.

MK1 GTI 1600 1976-1982

For a couple of reasons you will be unlikely to encounter a GTI built before the start of the 1980 model year.

Launched in the summer of 1976, the first GTIs to be seen in Britain started to filter through in the autumn of the same year. However, no provision had been made for export to a right-hand-drive country, and it would be the end of July 1979 for the '80 model year before this situation was rectified. By coincidence, it was at this point that Volkswagen began to offer a six year warranty against bodywork corrosion, earlier examples having lacked the protection necessary for longevity. Wax injection of cavities, plus bonded and sealed panel edges became the norm.

Mk1 GTI 1600 – pre 1979 model year.

GTIs built before 1983 were endowed with a 1588cc, 110bhp, fuel injected (Bosch K-Jetronic) engine. Bore and stroke stood at 79.5 x 80mm, compression at 9.5:1. Maximum torque of 103lb.ft was achieved at 5000rpm. 0-60mph was possible in 9.0 seconds via a four-speed box, while the top speed was declared to be 110mph.

Early GTIs sported 5.5x13in alloys, but these were soon replaced by steel wheels of the same size. 12-spoke alloys were introduced in 1980, and 9-spoke the following year. The 1979 model year saw the cheap-looking girder-style bumpers replaced with more stylish wraparound plastic ones. They linked neatly to the plastic wheelarch extensions essential to a GTI's sporty appearance. From early 1980 the GTI benefited from a five-speed close ratio gearbox, the effect of which was a claimed 0-60 sprint in 8.8 seconds and a top speed of 112mph.

● x500 for a runner to ● x5000 for a Concours rarity – beware rust on pre '79s.

MK1 GTI 1800 1983

An upgraded 1800 Mk1 GTI was introduced to the UK market in November 1982, only nine months before the Mk2 Golf was due for launch in Germany. This is the Mk1 that you are most likely to encounter at shows, or even on the roads.

Designed to give both better fuel economy and greater low speed torque, the 1781cc engine had an enlarged bore of 81mm and a longer stroke of 86.4mm compared to the 1600. Larger valves, longer conrods, a new crankshaft and lighter pistons were amongst the other changes made. Maximum power rose only slightly, up from 110 to 112bhp, but was achieved at lower revs, 5800 per minute.

Maximum torque was 109lb.ft, a figure which was achieved at just 3500rpm. Volkswagen claimed a top speed of 114mph for the 1800 engine, and a 0-60mph time of 8.2 seconds. The fact that the 1800 could run on unleaded fuel is a reasonably important consideration today.

Mk1 GTI 1800 – in Campaign guise, 1983.

The 1800 had a five-speed gearbox, but its gearing was higher than the 1600, so full advantage might be taken of the increase in torque at lower revs. An additional goody came in the form of the first MFA trip computer.

In Germany, May 1983, a special GTI with a four-lamp grille, 6x14in Pirelli alloys shod with 185/60 tyres, tinted glass, a sunroof, leather-trimmed steering wheel, and colour-coded bumpers, was introduced as a run-out model. Although lacking the luxury of colour-coding, a similar model was added to the UK listing in August. Mechanically identical to the standard GTI, this vehicle, known by enthusiasts as the Campaign GTI, was probably produced until December 1983, with some examples still available in the showrooms well into 1984. The Mk1 GTI wasn't available as a five-door model in the UK.

● x500 for a reasonable runner to ● x5000 for a Concours 1800: more desirable, better build quality and more readily available than the 1600.

Mk2 GTI 8-valve 1983/4-1991

The Mk2 Golf GTI made its debut in the UK in the spring of 1984. A bigger, more spacious, but consequently heavier car than the one it replaced, the Mk2 GTI inherited most of the attributes of the Campaign model, including a twin headlamp grille and, for a start, the famous Pirelli alloys, as well as comfort zone goodies such as internally adjustable door mirrors. Genuine improvements included superior suspension and better brakes; drums at the rear having been cast aside in favour of 226mm solid discs. Extra cost options took the GTI further upmarket and included central locking, electric windows and power-steering. Importantly, when considering buying a car of this age, Volkswagen claimed to have improved rust proofing, not only with wax and pre-treatment of metal, but also through advancement in manufacturing techniques.

Mk2 8v – run-out specification, late 1991.

In part thanks to a drag coefficient improvement of some 19 per cent, the 80kg increase in weight melted away. The Mk2 GTI had a top speed of 119mph, although the 0-62mph figure of 9.7 seconds quoted by Volkswagen made the car appear considerably slower because the previous 8.2 second figure was actually calculated on a 0-60mph time. Thanks to various tweaks, maximum torque had improved – standing at 115lb.ft at 3100rpm.

With the arrival of a five-door model for UK buyers in 1985, steel wheels became standard on the three-door model, although, at least for a time, alloys were part of the more expensive car's package. Hydraulic tappets became part of the package in 1986, but, more significantly, in 1987 Digifant Electronic Management replaced the continuous injection K-Jetronic system. The result was a slight increase in torque, up to 117lb.ft, though only at a higher figure of 4000rpm, but the fact that the car could run on ordinary 95-octane unleaded fuel was particularly important. For the 1990 model year, larger bumpers, foglamps as standard, and different side and wheelarch trims all helped to upgrade the vehicle's looks, while making it appear lower to the ground. In its final months the Mk2 GTI 8-valve was allocated electric windows and BBS alloys as standard – previously the preserve of the more powerful of the Mk2 GTIs, the 16-valve.

No need to bother with runners yet. Plenty of good and cheapish examples about. ● x950 will buy a reasonable car, ● x2500 an excellent stock GTI, but would anybody pay over ●x4000 for a Concours winning vehicle?

Mk2 GTI 16-valve 1985-1991

Although offered in left-hand-drive form for domestic consumption from 1985, the 16-valve GTI only became available for the UK market in 1987. Its purpose was clear; the GTI's position as leader of an ever increasing field of hot hatches was under threat. The advanced technology behind the 16-valve widened the gap once more and, as such, makes it a particularly desirable model today.

Considerably more powerful than the 8-valve, the engine was fitted with a new crossflow cylinder-head and twin camshafts. Two 32mm inlet and two 28mm exhaust valves per cylinder resulted in around 20 per cent more

Mk2 16v – two-door model.

gas flow. Maximum power of 139bhp was achieved at 6100rpm and peak torque of 123.5lb.ft at 4600rpm. Volkswagen claimed a top speed of 129mph and a 0-60mph sprint of 7.9 seconds.

Initially only available as a two-door, a four-door version was added in 1990 and the car ran on 6x14in Montreal alloys shod with 185/60 tyres. Later, 6x15in cross-spoke BBS rims and 185/55-15 tyres became the norm. The 16-valve sat 10mm lower than its 8-valve sibling. Body updates already outlined for the 8-valve were also applicable to the 16-valve.

The more powerful and desirable 16-valve attracts higher prices than the 8-valve. You might expect to pay ⬤ x4000 for a top notch car, but for ⬤ x5000 there should be another vehicle somewhere that's cheaper.

Rallye Golf

Regarded by most as the ultimate Mk2, production, all of which dates from 1989, was restricted to 5000 examples; the minimum required for motorsport homologation. Although the Rallye Golf was only manufactured in left-hand-drive guise, 80 examples were specifically set aside for the UK market, while others have found their way into the country over the years.

Rallye Golf – 5000-only motorsport special.

The engine was in essence, based on that of the eight-valve GTI with Digifant injection. However, the bore was reduced from 81mm to 80.6mm, which in turn decreased the displacement from 1781cc to 1763cc. This ensured that when the 1.4 multiplication factor was applied to forced induction – a requirement in motorsport – the Rallye Golf came under the 2.5-litre class limit. The car's G60 supercharger ran at 1.7 times the engine speed, delivering a maximum boost of 0.65bar (9.4psi). A substantial intercooler reduced the inlet air temperature by anything up to 55ºC. Maximum power of 160bhp was achieved at 5600rpm, while peak torque of 166lb.ft occurred at 4000rpm, although 150lb.ft was available between 2500 and 5600rpm. Volkswagen quoted a top speed of 130mph and a 0-60 sprint time of 7.6 seconds. The Rallye ran on premium unleaded fuel.

The Rallye Golf also featured Volkswagen's Syncro system, a five-speed gearbox specifically designed for a four-wheel drive function, plus suspension lowered by 20mm, fitted with stiffer springs and dampers, and fully independent at the rear. The Syncro system centred round a viscous coupling which was mounted a little ahead of the rear differential. This transmitted drive to the rear wheels at the point when the front wheels started to lose grip and began to spin.

Power-steering was standard, as was ABS. 280mm vented discs were fitted on the front wheels, while at the rear the Rallye carried Polo front discs and Golf callipers. The car featured 6x15in Sebring alloys shod with 205/50 tyres.

Particularly noteworthy is the Rallye Golf's unique bodyshell, which included extended wheelarches constructed out of steel, wide sill panels, plus a special grille with distinctive rectangular headlamps, bigger bumpers than normal, and a deep front spoiler with built in foglamps. The interior was also different to the standard GTI specification.

Rarity, status and the car's following ensure that the Rallye could fetch as much as ⬤ x6500, but we think ⬤ x7000 is over the top. If one on offer is cheap – say ⬤ x4500 to ⬤ x5000 – ask why.

Golf GTI G60

The G60 went on sale in mainland Europe in December 1989, available as three- or five-door, and remained a mainstream model until production of the Mk2 in general ceased in July 1991. Although a front-wheel-drive vehicle in standard form, Volkswagen added a Syncro version of the G60 in February 1991. Never imported officially to the UK, a reasonable number of examples are seen at Volkswagen shows, making the car well worth including in our Buyers Guide.

Mk2 GTI G60 – supercharged LHD production model.

Unlike the Rallye, the G60 had the normal displacement of 1781cc. Compared to the standard 8-valve on which the engine was based, compression was reduced to 8:1 while the supercharger remained the same as that bolted onto the Rallye Golf. High levels of torque demanded that the MQ gearbox fitted to the Passat and Corrado be installed, as with the Rallye, but in this instance, fifth gear was longer. Suspension, lowered by 20mm at the front and 10mm at the rear, was comparable to that of the 16-valve GTI. Early examples were supplied with 6x15in steel wheels, but later, in August 1990, the previously optional 6.5x15in BBS alloys became standard. Like the Rallye, the G60 ran on premium unleaded fuel.

With the exception of the front wings which, although conventionally-shaped, were wider than those of the eight- and 16-valve GTI, the rest of the bodywork and the interior trim was the same as that of the 16-valve model.

The lack of four-wheel-drive made the standard G60 lighter than the Rallye, but it was, nevertheless, heavier than the 16-valve. Volkswagen quoted a figure of 8.3 seconds for the 0-62mph sprint and a top speed of 134mph, making it marginally faster than the 16-valve even with the quirks of gauging performance in different guises removed. Crucially, the G60 had more torque throughout the range.

Super fast, but a left hooker and doesn't have quite the rarity value of the Rallye. You are most likely to encounter one of these where the owner knows you will be prepared to pay some sort of premium – just as he no doubt did! Aim to pay ● x4500 for one, but expect an owner not to drop below ● x5250.

The Cabriolet Golf

Introduced in 1979, there were no major changes made, either in its appearance or build, during the Cabriolet's 13-year lifespan. Built for Volkswagen by Karmann at its factory in Osnabrück, the Cabriolet's hood, like that of its soft-top Beetle predecessor, was virtually without equal. Comprised of five separate layers of cloth, insulation, and waterproof plastics, the hood also featured a head-lining comparable to that of the tin-top hatch, along with a heated glass rear window.

The hood contributed to a substantial reduction in boot space, with only 9.9cu.ft available when the rear seat was in position. A rollover hoop helped to maintain rigidity, as did an extra cross-member beneath the dashboard, and deeper sills.

A GTI version of the Cabriolet was available throughout, although for some years the car was badged as a GLi. The Cabriolet was given a makeover for the '87 model year with a bodykit encompassing big bumpers with integral spoiler lips, and sculptured sills that tied in well with the extended wheelarches. Better still, everything was colour-coded.

Special editions, including the Quartet and the CC, and near run-out models such as the Sportline and Rivage, added extra goodies in terms of trim and special alloy wheels, remaining the most sought after of any Golf Cabriolet.

Cabrio Golf GTI CC special edition.

There's definitely interest in the Golf Cabrio, however, a genuine GTI enthusiast is unlikely to be hooked by the thought of a soft top, while those with real money might be taken by an Eos straight from the showroom. A tasty ready to show late model special edition might edge towards ● x6500 – but if the hood has had it, bargain down in an ever decreasing circle. Realistically expect to pay ● x2000 for a solid but tired car wanting a bit of work and lots of TLC.

5 Before you view
– be well informed

To avoid a wasted journey, and the disappointment of finding that a Mk1 or Mk2 GTI does not match your expectations, it will help if you're very clear about what questions you want to ask before you pick up the telephone. Some of these points might appear basic but, when you're excited about the prospect of buying, some of the most obvious things can slip the mind. Also check the current values of the model you are interested in by thumbing through the specialist Volkswagen magazines and publications such as *Autotrader*.

Where is the Golf?
Is it going to be worth travelling two or three hundred miles? A locally advertised Golf, although it may not sound very interesting, can add to your knowledge for very little effort, so make a visit – it might even be in better condition than expected.

Dealer or private sale?
Establish early on if the Golf is being sold by its owner or by a trader. A private owner should have all the history, so don't be afraid to ask detailed questions. A dealer may have more limited knowledge of a car's history but should have some documentation. A dealer may offer a warranty/guarantee (ask for a printed copy) and finance.

Cost of collection and delivery
A dealer may well be used to quoting for delivery by transporter. A private owner may agree to meet you halfway, but only agree to this after you have seen the Golf at the vendor's address to validate the documents. Conversely, you could meet halfway and agree the sale but insist on meeting at the vendor's address for the handover.

View – when and where?
It is always preferable to view at the vendor's home or business premises. In the case of a private sale, the Golf's documentation should tally with the vendor's name and address. Arrange to view in daylight and avoid a wet day. Any car is likely to look better in poor light or when wet.

Reason for sale?
Do make it one of the first questions. Why is the Golf being sold and how long has it been with the current owner? How many previous owners?

Left-hand-drive to right-hand-drive
Although some Golfs on the market were originally prepared for another country, or were never available in RHD form, it's unusual to find one that has been switched from LHD. If professionally executed the work would have proved costly, if carried out in a back-yard there is a possibility that the changeover could be amateurish in nature. Common sense would advise keeping clear of such vehicles. Generally, steering conversions can only reduce the value.

Condition (body/chassis/interior/mechanicals)

Ask for an honest appraisal of the Golf's condition. Ask specifically about some of the check items described in chapter 7.

All original specification?

An original specification Golf GTI won't necessarily command a higher value than an upgraded model unless it is in absolutely pristine Concours condition. However, if a car is non-standard it is important to glean more about the work carried out, with specific reference to technical competence, receipted invoices and, in many instances, photographic records.

Matching data/legal ownership

Do VIN/chassis, engine numbers and licence plate match the official registration document? Is the owner's name and address recorded in the official registration documents?

For those countries that require an annual test of roadworthiness, does the Golf have a document showing it complies (an MoT certificate in the UK, which can be verified on 0845 600 5977)? If a smog/emissions certificate is mandatory, does the Golf have one?

If required, does the Golf carry a current road fund licence/licence plate tag? Does the vendor own the Golf outright? Money might be owed to a finance company or bank: the Golf could even be stolen. Several organisations will supply the data on ownership, based on the Golf's license plate number, for a fee. Such companies can often also tell you whether the car has been 'written off' by an insurance company. In the UK, the organisations listed below can supply vehicle data:

HPI – 01722 422 422
AA – 0870 600 0836
DVLA – 0870 240 0010
RAC – 0870 533 3660
Other countries will have similar organisations.

Unleaded fuel

If the car you are looking at is fitted with a catalytic converter, unleaded fuel **must** be used. A 'cat' was listed as an option from 1990, but may also be present if a transplanted engine from a later car (2ltr 16v Seat Cupra engines are a popular choice) has been used. All GTIs benefit from using 98RON fuel but is an essential requirement for a 16v, G60 or Rallye. However, 16v engines built for the US market can be run on 95RON fuel, but are down on power by 10bhp SAE.

Insurance

It's best never to take risks with something like insurance. Arrange everything in advance with your company or broker and, if required, give further details over the phone should you decide to buy. Remember that with classic insurance there's the benefit of agreed value, if the Golf is not going to be your only vehicle.

How can you pay?

A cheque/check will take several days to clear and the seller may prefer to sell to a cash buyer. However, a banker's draft (a cheque issued by a bank) is a good as cash, but safer, so contact your own bank and become familiar with the formalities that are necessary to obtain one.

Buying at auction?
If the intention is to buy at auction see chapter 10 for further advice.

Professional vehicle check (mechanical examination)
There are often marque/model specialists who will undertake professional examination of a vehicle on your behalf. Owners' clubs will be able to put you in touch with such specialists and may even offer the service themselves.

Other organisations that will carry out a general professional check in the UK are:

AA – 0800 085 3007 (motoring organisation with vehicle inspectors)
ABS – 0800 358 5855 (specialist vehicle inspection company)
RAC – 0870 533 3660 (motoring organisation with vehicle inspectors)
Other countries will have similar organisations.

6 Inspection equipment
– these items will really help

This book
Reading glasses (if you need them for close work)
Magnet (not powerful, a fridge magnet is ideal)
Torch
Probe (a small screwdriver works very well)
Overalls
Mirror on a stick
Digital camera
A friend, preferably a knowledgeable enthusiast

Before you rush out of the door, gather together a few items that will help as you work your way around the proposed Golf. This book is designed to be your guide at every step, so take it along and use the check boxes to help you assess each area of the Golf you're interested in. Don't be afraid to let the seller see you using it.

Take your reading glasses if you need them to read documents and make close-up inspections.

A magnet will help you check if the Golf is full of filler, although even a light skim can be dangerous in the long-term. However, even professional body-shops use a skim of filler to achieve the final result when repairing accident damage. Use the magnet to sample bodywork areas all around the Golf, particularly the lower sections and the tops of the front wings in the case of the Mk1, but be careful not to damage the paintwork. Ideally, there won't be any filler, but you might find a little here and there, just not whole panels.

A torch with fresh batteries will be useful for peering behind the wheels and around the suspension and exhaust system of the Golf. It might even be useful in the engine compartment and for viewing the electrical components under the dashboard.

A small blunt screwdriver can be used – with care – as a probe, particularly under the sills, around the jacking points, and on any exposed metal in the vicinity of the wheelarches. With this you should be able to check for an area of severe corrosion, but be careful – if it's really bad the screwdriver might go right through the metal! (We suggest permission should be sought before you probe and, if it isn't granted and there's no explanation that you walk away).

Be prepared to get dirty. Take along a pair of overalls, if you have them. Fixing a mirror at an angle on the end of a stick may seem odd, but when examining Golf exhaust systems and other hidden components this can be useful, even if you have taken our advice and made sure you crawl right under the Golf to see for yourself. A mirror will also help you to peer into the out of the way crevices around the engine and transmission.

If you have the use of a digital camera, take it along so that later you can study some areas of the Golf more closely. Take pictures of any part of the car that causes you concern, and seek expert opinion.

Ideally, have a friend or knowledgeable enthusiast accompany you: a second opinion is always valuable.

7 Fifteen minute evaluation
– walk away or stay?

This is our quick but crucial guide. If the car fails here, there's no point proceeding to the more detailed evaluation.

Exterior

Before you go any further, if you are looking at a Mk1, check, with the aid of your mirror, the condition of the metal tube between the petrol filler cap and the tank. If rusty, small particles of corrosion have entered the tank, they will eventually cause expensive damage to the Bosch K-Jetronic fuel injection unit. If you are exceptionally lucky, you may find a car with an aftermarket stainless steel filler neck tube!

A thorough examination of the petrol filler pipe on a Mk1 could save you years of grief with the fuel injection system.

Pre '80 Golf; most have long since crumbled to dust.

The Rallye Golf has many unique panels, including extended wheelarches and side skirts, all of which are formed out of steel.

With the exception of Golfs built before the 1980 model year, you are unlikely to be looking at terminal rust as VW's body protection is good. If the car is rusty, walk away – there are plenty other cars available; and if it's a Rallye Golf, think how much sorting out a car with unique panels is going to cost, and then walk away! Badly repaired accident damage can cause rust, years of neglect often does too – walk away. But what about a sound Cabriolet with a rotten hood? Even then we'd be inclined to walk away. If a hood's not watertight, what hidden damage might have been caused? Again, there are still plenty of cars available.

As for a pre '80 Golf, most have long since crumbled to dust. Find one that hasn't and you are in luck, but do check it out for the proverbial filler and other tricks employed before you go for a serious evaluation. With step-by-step photographic evidence, a fully restored early GTI is worth snapping up.

Check the condition of the mechanism and catches on a Cabriolet hood. Examine the hood fabric for signs of leaking. Untold damage may have been done to the interior if the hood is rotten.

Sound body, but with faded paintwork and tired plastic? T-cut, including that specifically for metallic finishes, and proprietary cosmetic products can work wonders. It's worth going to the next stage.

Heavily curbed alloys? Decent replacements won't be cheap, while a full refurbishment is just as pricey! It's a bargaining tool rather than an outright deterrent to purchasing.

Sound body, but with faded paintwork and tired plastic? T-cut, including that specifically for metallic finishes, and proprietary cosmetic products can work wonders.

Interior

If originality is the great goal in life, a generally below par interior can be difficult to rectify.

It should be feasible, but not necessarily cheap, to replace a torn and otherwise scarred head-lining. Upholstery patterns varied over the years and, as all are cloth and inevitably age, sunlight, sharp objects in pockets and more will have taken their toll. Speaking to those who restored a GTI, some have come across just what they wanted, but you are likely to struggle to do the same. Worn carpets can be replaced. As long as the plastics aren't physically scarred or cracked, they can be brought back to life. The biggest walk away of the lot has to be soggy dripping carpets – easy enough to replace, but that solves nothing.

With the exceptions noted above – the Rallye and the earliest of GTIs – the cars are sufficiently plentiful that it shouldn't be necessary to go to the toil and trouble of remedial interior work. View another car.

The interior shown is from the earliest known Mk1 GTI and is in excellent condition. Shabby, torn upholstery and damaged door cards can be difficult to replace – if originality is the aim.

Mechanicals

Most components are readily available and at an affordable price, except if you are looking at a Rallye or G60 where model specific items such as the supercharger and parts for the all-wheel-drive system could be rare and pricey.

Look under the bonnet of the Golf. The engine should be clean – but not overly so on all but a Concours car – and well cared for. Can you see everything you would expect? Many GTIs have been modified, so it's likely you will find some non-standard components. The air-filter might well have been replaced by a cone type such as K&N, while upper, and sometimes lower, strut braces could have been fitted to improve the steering response during hard cornering. Check that the exhaust down-pipe heat shield is in place, as the heat from this part of the system can burn the paint off the bulkhead, leading to rust and an expensive repair. Finally, inspect the inner wings for evidence of accident damage.

Don't forget to look for oil leaks. While a slight dribble of oil in the vicinity of the sump gasket or the cam cover isn't a problem, lots of oil leaking from the join between the cylinder head and the engine block, saturating the alternator, is indicative of a defective cylinder head gasket that could prove to be expensive to rectify. Remember to check the fuel system for leaks around the connections.

Ask the vendor to start the GTI while you watch the exhaust. A little smoke on starting up is acceptable, providing it quickly settles down to a nice even tick-over with no visible fumes.

Are there any knocking noises when the engine speed increases? The causes are numerous, but all could spell trouble in the future. Ignore minor tappet noises, as a slightly loose tappet is better than a tight, very quiet one on any engine. The engines fitted to Mk2 GTIs benefit from hydraulic tappets which can tap away for several minutes after the engine is started. However, should the noise persist, replacement will be necessary.

Dating from 1987 or after, this Mk2 8-valve engine features Digifant Electronic Management.

Check: edges of wheelarches where arch protectors are riveted to wings; rust on door bottoms, step and lower edge between the outer and inner sill; window seals, door mirrors, wheels and tyres; difficult to source waistline trim and early metal bumper end caps on Mk1; condition of plastic rubbing strips and bumpers Mk2; metal petrol filler pipe and cap on Mk1.

Examine: front edge of bonnet and front wings for stone chips, also strip of metal above front bumper, front edge of roof, under windscreen, especially wiper spindle exit points; grille and spoiler assembly under bumper for accident damage; also condition of light units and reflectors.

Early Mk1 Golfs are particularly rust-prone. Examine the panel between spare wheel well and rear valance, and around lock barrel. Weak point of Mk2 is tailgate: check bottom edge, around number plate and bump-stops. All models check lower edge of rear valance, panel seams and badges.

Confirm installed engine is correct for model. Check condition of: radiator, hoses, and ancillaries. Look for evidence of oil leaks, particularly head gasket oil leaking onto alternator. Examine engine wiring. Be suspicious if non-standard wires appear to bypass components. Engines of modified Golfs will be adorned with many non-original components.

Check condition of: head-linings, seats and carpets; under carpets and over-mats if fitted for damp; dashboard for damage. Make sure all functions of instrument panel, including MFA computer, are working.

Underside – Mk1 Scirocco illustrated, Mk1 Golf similar. Check all points indicated; 1. Sills 2. Front sub frame and steering components 3. Drive-shaft joints and gaiters 4. Shock absorbers and coil springs 5. Engine oil, transmission oil and coolant leaks 6. Rear axle mounting points. 7. Fuel and brake lines.

9 Serious evaluation
– 60 minutes for years of enjoyment

Exterior
Paint

Ex Gd Av Po
[4] [3] [2] [1]

Volkswagen paint is legendary and lasts for years. However, T-cut works wonders, particularly if you are dealing with colours like red, which, unless lovingly polished on a regular basis, fades fast. There are special cutting polishes for metallic paint, but we aren't quite as convinced here. Look out for a re-sprayed panel, a full new coat of paint, slap-dash, quick tidy-up work, etc. – paint on trim, plastic or rubber. Check for a paint job that might be mismatched – it will annoy you! Think that if you go to a professional for a tidy-up job, the bill will be big if you are to avoid some of the issues contained in Chapter 14.

Minor scratches and scuffs – aftermarket or specialist paint companies can usually solve the problem of a touch up spray, if a dealer finds the colour to be obsolete. Also don't rule out operations specialising in the removal of stone chips, etc. One company we approached refused to touch a silver car!

If it's a customised Golf in rice pudding and jam puce, think whether anybody else except you will like it if you come to sell.

Years of neglect have caused the paint to fade, with red being particularly prone to this.

Panels

Ex Gd Av Po
[4] [3] [2] [1]

Rust! Having established that we are going to walk away unless it's a rare model, and even then we might hesitate before putting in a bid, where is the rust likely to be?

Mk1
Rotten fuel filler neck (this is reasonably serious as corroded flakes of metal can fall into the fuel tank and the next you know it's cough, spit, splutter); rotting tailgate edges and around the lock, (you won't get a new tailgate from Volkswagen, but should be able to pick up a second-hand example); metal sunroofs might rust along the edges and drain holes get blocked, leading to water problems and, worst case scenario, holes in the metal follow (don't go there – please!). Check the lower corners of the windscreen area – rust breeds under the windscreen rubber and then spreads along the scuttle – the worse it is the more serious the consequences become. Catch it early and keep an eye

The fuel filler neck, seen here behind the right-hand rear suspension unit, can create serious problems for the fuel injection system if found to be corroded. Due to the extensive use of plastic for the fuel filler pipe and the tank, this is not a problem on Mk2 models.

on it thereafter and you'll be alright. But if the rust has spread, this means major restoration work.

Door bottoms and wheelarches! Blocked drain holes tend to be the cause of rust with the former. If it has got as far as being visible on the outside edge of the door, buy a replacement door. Wheelarches come in for a battering from salt and road detritus, and aren't helped by the self-tapping screws securing the plastic liners in place. To us, if wheelarch edges haven't been kept in check – it's a telltale sign of less than conscientious housekeeping – delve more deeply elsewhere!

While checking for corrosion around the unique Mk1 filler cap, it's worth noting that the swage line trim seen below, along with other external trim, is becoming increasingly difficult to find.

Corrosion can form around the tailgate lock on Mk1 models.

Door bottoms are prone to rust problems, usually due to blocked drain holes and worn window scraper rubbers. Creeping rust can also spread to the front wing from under the plastic arch protector.

Exposed wheelarches can become frayed at the edges due to grit and debris thrown up from the wheels.

Crawl underneath to check the jacking points, and for factory under-seal or the lack of it, examine the panel jointing between the spare wheel well and the rear panel. Rot is common here. Also, check the underside of the rear wing for signs of corrosion around the filler neck.

Mk2

Sunroofs can be an issue again, as can tailgates and the front edge of the bonnet, while notes on windscreen rubbers and rust accumulation prevalent on Mk1s are pertinent to the newer car. The area surrounding the left-hand wiper spindle needs checking.

Underneath the car, it's a case of looking at the seam where the floor panel

The air deflector for the sunroof often corrodes and affects the surrounding metal.

meets the sills, and the outer sill where it meets the inner at the lowest point – and this is an important one. Also check for rust in the bulkhead area, caused by heat from the exhaust manifold burning off paint and protection, and again have a look at the jack mounting points.

The area around the tailgate bump stop is vulnerable to corrosion.

This Mk2 rear valance has corroded around the towing eye and the panel join.

The front edge of the bonnet and all forward facing panels are vulnerable to stone chips.

The pressing for the left-hand wiper spindle is particularly prone to corrosion on the Mk2.

From below, it's a case of looking at the seam where the floor panel meets the sills, the lower lip and jacking points.

As far as replacement panels go for both the Mk1 and Mk2, Volkswagen would say, if it still has what you want, that these are better than an aftermarket version. It might say that – we couldn't possibly comment! Assuming a panel (genuine or otherwise) has been fitted, does it really fit? If no, and it's not a rare model, let the vendor sell the car elsewhere. Also, even if it's a good fit, ask why it's happened. Is it concealing badly repaired accident damage?

Ex [4]   Gd [3]   Av [2]   Po [1]

Shut lines

We can think of one Golf where the driver's door had dropped so much that he had to lift it back in place every time it was closed. We think not! Do bad shut lines indicate accident damage? – check out this one more closely.

Wide panel gaps may indicate poorly repaired accident damage, or the dubious fit of aftermarket replacement panels.

Exterior trim

Truth to tell we are looking at an era when shiny trim was deemed distinctly out of date. Black plastic bumpers and trim inserts grey with age and lack of attention, but can be brought back to life with proprietary cleaners and polishes. Paint overspray is a pain; polish marks can be removed with white spirit if you persevere. Vinyl trim around the rear window of a Mk1 isn't available as a re-orderable item; neither are the vinyl trim lines on the lower door and rear quarter panels. However, any self respecting sign maker can sort these two out for you. Badges are vulnerable to lowlife attack and pillage – fortunately, replacements can be picked up reasonably easy.

Mk2, check exterior trim, such as rubbing strips and wheelarch trims, for damage. Grey, faded trim can usually be resurrected with cleaning products or the careful application of heat.

The vinyl trim around the rear window of a Mk1 can deteriorate with age. Now an obsolete part, it can be replicated by a sign making company.

The fixing holes are often the culprit for rust appearing around the badges.

The chrome on this tailgate badge has worn through, exposing the grey plastic base. Note the bottom edge of the tailgate is beginning to corrode.

Wipers

Inevitably, numerous variations of wiper-blade and arm have been produced over the years. Some owners have converted the original two-blade system to one with a single arm and blade. A sluggish action would indicate that the wiper spindles have ingested water and road grit and are about to seize up. The rear wiper can also be a troublesome beast. Failure can be due to a seized wiper spindle, or broken wires in the rubber tube fitted between the body and the tailgate. The latter can also affect the operation of the number plate lights and, while it's not a walk away situation, it can be a very fiddly task to reconnect the wires.

A sluggish wiper action indicates that the wiper spindles have ingested water and road grit and are about to seize up. Some owners convert the original two-blade system to one with a single arm and blade.

The rear wiper spindle is also vulnerable to seizing due to ingesting road grit and moisture.

Sunroof

Ex | Gd | Av | Po
4 | 3 | 2 | 1

All sunroofs can leak as age makes them less serviceable – while aftermarket tilting glass fittings might be a pain from the word go. Watch out for stained upholstery due to water ingress as a tell tale sign and beware, the stains don't come out easily, while there will be a big bill elsewhere! A rotten wind deflector panel can cause rust to spread into the surrounding sunroof aperture, while the seal around the opening panel can eventually rub through the paint, again encouraging rust to form.

An aftermarket glass sunroof panel is often a dubious fit, with the resulting leakage causing water damage to the interior.

These seats from a 1300 Mk2 Golf are stained due to water entering the car via the aftermarket sunroof.

Glass

Ex | Gd | Av | Po
4 | 3 | 2 | 1

We all know about scratched or chipped windscreens being a cause of potential failure of the British MoT test. Fortunately, glass for Mk1 and Mk2 Golfs is readily available in one form or another.

Check the laminated windscreen for opaque edges. The metal in the corner of the screen is corroding from under the rubber surround. This may be the tip of the iceberg with extensive perforated metal under the rubber, allowing water to drip on to the fuse box below.

Lights

Tarnished or rusted reflectors in any age of headlamp will result in test failure, but replacements are readily available for just about every model. Beware of auxiliary lights that have been fitted by someone inexperienced. We know of one car where the extra driving lamps were all connected to one fuse, resulting in burnt contacts and lights like candles. Fortunately, this was cured by wiring the lights through relays activated by the remaining good fuse.

Check the headlight reflectors aren't tarnished or corroded. Also, beware the aftermarket clear lens lights as most seem to deteriorate rapidly.

This many segmented rear light is of the type fitted to later Mk1 GTIs. All Mk1 and Mk2 lights are now advancing in years and the plastic is more brittle. Check the condition and fixing tabs of the bulb insert from inside the boot.

The original rear lights fitted to the Mk2 are of good quality and only need checking for accident damage or problems with the bulb holder.

Smoked lenses were a factory fitment for some later models, while coloured lenses are a favourite of the custom fraternity.

So-called 'Lexus style' rear lights seen on the Mk2 are a custom fitment; likewise the 8v badge.

There are several variations in Mk1 rear lights, while the Mk2 retained the same design throughout its life. However, a lot of owners have opted to fit coloured or smoked lenses, while some Mk2 cars had the latter fitted at the factory.

Front indicator lenses are also a target for the custom brigade, often being changed to clear or smoked lenses and fitted with an amber bulb. Most Concours judges will turn a blind eye to this, unless the unit fitted is particularly obnoxious.

Ex   Gd   Av   Po
[4]   [3]   [2]   [1]

The original Mk1 GTI left the factory fitted with 5.5Jx13in steel wheels shod with 175/70HR rated radial-ply tyres. Later the Mk1 was offered with alloy wheels, albeit the same size as the steels. The Mk1 Campaign model came equipped with 6Jx14in Pirelli alloys, while the Mk2 GTI debuted with 6Jx14in wheels fitted with 185/60HR rated tyres. The 16v Mk2 sported 6Jx15in BBS alloys equipped with 185/55 tyres. When the G60 arrived on the scene, 6Jx15in alloys were provided, fitted with 185/55 rubber. The competition orientated Rallye Golf was fitted with 6Jx15in Sebring alloys, but this time fitted with 205/50 boots.

Check that the GTI you are viewing has the wheels Volkswagen intended. If it hasn't, is this what you really want? You are likely to find a huge variety of non-standard wheel types and sizes up to 17in on the Mk1, and 18in on the Mk2. We feel that Volkswagen's extensive research to find the correct wheel and tyre size for each model, based on average driving styles and comfort level, is most appropriate. While this can be improved upon slightly, there is also the danger of producing both a bouncy ride and below par handling. Check that the Golf you are viewing has sufficient clearance under the wings to allow full steering movement without fouling the bodywork. Be aware that you may find that both the wings and wheelarches have been butchered to accommodate outrageously bigger wheel and tyre combinations. Check the wheels for damage. Buckled rims may mean that the Golf has 'clouted' the curb, which in turn could have damaged suspension components. Are the wheels rusty, or is there evidence of repainting? Steel wheels are notorious for rust damage and badly pitted ones are difficult to restore to factory standard. Curbed alloys, apart from being unsightly, are costly to have refurbished.

Check that the tyres are all of the same type. A mix and match of makes will lose points in any Concours and isn't ideal elsewhere.

Mk1 with 5.5Jx13in steel wheels shod with 175/70HR.

Mk1 with 5.5Jx13in alloy wheels shod with 175/70HR.

The steel wheels offered as standard on the three-door Mk2 GTI.

The last edition Mk1 Campaign model came equipped with 6Jx14in Pirelli alloys. This style of wheel was also offered as an option on the early Mk2 GTI.

6Jx15in BBS alloys equipped with 185/55 tyres, as fitted to the 16v and run-out Mk2 8v GTI.

The competition orientated Rallye Golf was fitted with 6Jx15in Sebring alloys, shod with 205/50 tyres.

Hub bearings and steering joints, steering rack

Ex Gd Av Po

4 3 2 1

The front wheel bearings become noisy when worn, and this will be apparent during the course of the road test. Noise will be noticeable when the car is driven in a straight line, but the car may be quieter when turning a corner. With the front of the Golf safely supported on axle stands, grip the wheel at both top and bottom and rock it. If there is play, it could be wear in the bottom link ball joint at the foot of the suspension strut. This may cause a strange sensation through the steering when changing direction if the play is excessive. The rear mounting point of the front wishbone can give a similar sensation when worn to excess. Check that the ball joints on the trackrods are free of excessive play. (MoT stations use a pry bar to check the condition of the various ball joints, so if you are in any doubt, it might be prudent to enlist the help of your friendly tester.)

With the steering in the straight-ahead position, turn the steering wheel left and right. There should be no movement before the wheels start to move. Play is indicative of a steering rack that needs replacing.

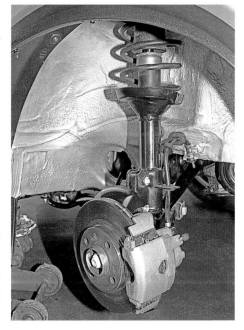

This Mk1 strut is in excellent condition; examine springs for breakage and the damper for leakage. Don't forget to check the dampers by pressing down on each corner of the car to detect excessive bounce.

Interior
Seats

You won't find a Mk1 GTI or a Mk2 with vinyl upholstery, so at least you won't be stuck to the seat. You will find both generations with a variety of patterns of upholstery dependent on the age. Sadly, cloth wears out more quickly than plastic because it isn't as robust. The driver seat bolsters, and particularly the one close to the door, can often be beyond repair. Seat reupholstering isn't cheap if it is any good. Getting hold of the original fabric, or a really close copy is a nightmare, while a second-hand seat from a scrapyard is likely to suffer the same kind of problems. If it's not a Concours car, why not pay out for a decent upholstery of your choice, if it is ... keep your fingers crossed; we know of one chap in Norfolk who just happened to be in the right place at the right time!

The Rallye Golf has a leather/fabric combination trim. If the leather is OK, it means someone has fed it with conditioning cream over the years.

Stained or grubby upholstery can be cleaned, but beware, for a decent result this is no five minute job. Go for a suitable brand – and do read the instructions.

The driver's seat bolsters, particularly the one close to the door, can often be beyond repair.

The Rallye Golf has a leather/fabric combination trim.

Carpets

Beware of damp carpets; replacements won't solve the problem. Dirty carpets, on the other hand, can be cleaned, and it's not even necessary to call in the professionals. Worn carpets, particularly those in the driver's foot well can be replaced with reasonable copies, and think over-mats for future preservation purposes. Unless they are wet, we wouldn't be put off from purchasing by undesirable carpets.

Head-lining

There's quite a bit of black around when it comes to the GTI version of the Golf's head-lining. This helps if the car has been in the hands of a smoker. Rips and tears are rips and tears no matter what the material. Some owners fit new head-linings themselves – but tend to curse a good deal. Availability is reasonable. The Mk2 has a solid head-lining that is more robust, though the cloth used around the sunroof aperture is also prone to tearing if repairs to the mechanism become necessary.

Door cards

Door cards generally don't cause problems; that is unless the plastic membrane behind the door has been punctured at some point. (The fitting of big speakers can be one cause, fitting a replacement window lifting mechanism might be another. Fortunately, the door lock can be replaced by just peeling back the membrane from the top corner and then sticking it back down). If the door card is warped, and worse still wet, chances are the carpets won't be perfect, and there will be that mouldy, musty smell from which it's best to walk way. Re-trimming a door is tedious – finding the right material with the correct mouldings isn't easy. Second-hand panels from the local scrapyard might be the answer.

The vinyl-covered door cards found on Mk1 models are less prone to water damage, but warping can occur.

Door cards generally don't cause problems; that is unless the plastic membrane behind the door has been punctured at some time, leading to staining, especially on the cloth-covered type fitted to Mk2 models.

Door locks and handles

In a word, robust, although any dodgy character intent on breaking into a Golf could make a mess of the panels around the lock. You may find that a caring owner has fitted armoured plates surrounding the lock mechanism end of the handle, to prevent the unwelcome attention of thieves, or to hide existing criminal damage. The door handles are robust and the proliferation of plastics means that corrosion isn't an issue either.

The armoured plate surrounding the lock mechanism end of the handle is an aftermarket fitment designed to prevent the unwelcome attention of thieves, or to hide existing criminal damage.

The door handles are fairly robust but an internal mechanism of non-original replacements can be of dubious quality.

Window winders

Yes, the winder, or at least the ratchet system behind it, can fail but it's not common. Electric windows, and we are thinking late Mk2 models mostly here, can suffer from dodgy motors, but nowhere near to the same extent as the comparatively youthful Mk4. An application of silicon spray can often free up a sluggish electric window, especially on the less-used passenger side of the car.

Steering wheel

Apart from some later standard designs being both decidedly dull and distinctly corporate, the steering wheel shouldn't be a problem. As for aftermarket steering wheels no larger than a decent coin of the realm, we're sufficiently boring enough to condemn them out of hand!

A percentage of Golfs have been fitted with aftermarket steering wheels. For Concours, originality is king. This wheel was fitted to late model Mk1 cars and some Mk2s.

Instrument panel

Ex Gd Av Po
4   3   2   1

We are talking plastic in a big way here. Providing there are no cracks or changes to the standard item which have employed hacksaw tactics, a dashboard will tidy up just like any other plastic. Regarding functions, if fitted with a dodgy MFA computer, there's a reasonable bill just around the corner, while if the heater control only works on the third position, the heater resistor pack fitted to the fan unit will have failed. Rumours of late model Mk2s going haywire abound; showing up initially as a loss of rev counter, oil and water lights, plus MFA computer functions. Full panel replacement is the only way forward – oh dear!

Providing the dashboard is intact and all the controls and instrument panel functions work, including the MFA computer, all is well.

Check that the rotary heater control operates in all positions. If only position 3 is working, the resistor pack on the fan unit has failed.

Handbrake

Ex Gd Av Po

All GTIs have a handbrake with separate cables to each rear wheel. If adjusted correctly, it should operate with a maximum of five to seven clicks. The Mk2 GTI is fitted with rear disc brakes and is more likely to suffer from handbrake problems, due to the exposed nature of the mechanism within the callipers. If the handbrake fails to hold the car, or the lever feels dead when pulled up, it's likely that the parking brake mechanism on the rear callipers has seized up. Dried-up lubrication and the ingress of dirt within the cables, and indeed a broken cable, can cause inefficient operation on all models.

Boot (trunk) interior/spare wheel and tool kit

Ex Gd Av Po

If the boot is wet, the most likely causes are a blocked sunroof drain tube, or a tailgate washer feed pipe that has become disconnected. The spare wheel well is under the boot lining material and is likely to be OK. It's always worth checking that there is a spare wheel in situ, and if it's in decent order. Negotiate with the vendor if the wheel is damaged or the tyre bordering on legal.

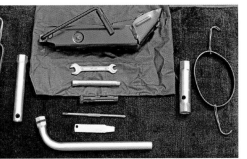

While most people possess sufficient tools to carry out emergency roadside repairs, the original toolkit is essential equipment for the Concours entrant.

Check the condition of the spare wheel, look for rust in the well, and, from under the car, the connecting panel between the well and the rear valance.

Mechanicals

Ex Gd Av Po

Under the bonnet – general impression

Is the engine clean, with everything in place? If the answer is yes, the chances are that it's been well looked after, or is a Concours car. If you find it covered in oil and road grime, then it's probably been neglected. Beware the car in only moderate condition with a newly cleaned engine: someone may be trying to disguise oil leaks, etc. With the engine switched off, grip the crankshaft pulley and check if it feels loose. If this is the case, the main crankshaft bolt has been undone by an inexperienced mechanic when changing the cam-belt, instead of undoing the four allen bolts that locate the outer pulley on its hub. The crankshaft bolt requires considerable torque to tighten it and this is virtually impossible in situ on an engine. A loose pulley can cause considerable damage to the end of the crankshaft and is a walk away item.

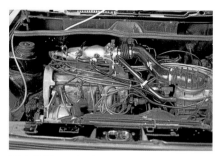
Mk1 1600 producing 110bhp.

Mk1 1800 engine with K-Jetronic injection, 112bhp.

Mk2 1800 8-valve, 112bhp.

Mk2 1800 16-valve, 139bhp.

Wiring

Ex	Gd	Av	Po
4	3	2	1

Look under the dashboard to find the bulk of the wiring. Although complicated to the eye, it's a fairly simple arrangement using foolproof multi-plugs with individually numbered contacts to connect components. The fuse-box and relay plate are also under the dashboard, with the fuses and relays numbered for ease of identification. (If you are just dismantling a component to work on the bodywork or the engine then it makes

Rallye Golf, 160bhp supercharged engine.

life simple as you are merely disconnecting a multi-plug.) Problems may arise if the metalwork around the window is perforated due to corrosion, as this can lead to water dripping onto the fuse-box and relay plate.

Are there lots of crimped, insulated spade connectors with gaudy red, blue or yellow insulation? This usually indicates trouble, especially if accompanied by a rat's nest of non-standard wiring colours. Worse still, you may find tap connectors (better known as 'Scotch-lock' connectors), and while these are great to get you home with a temporary repair, they invariably give trouble if used long term.

Under the bonnet the wiring loom also connects to the components with colour-coded multi-plugs. In areas of the engine bay where heat and oil could be present, the insulation often becomes brittle. Particularly prone to this problem is the important wire from the oil pressure warning light switch and other engine sensors. The voltage regulator is an integral part of the brush assembly on the alternator and is fairly straightforward to change, should the need arise. The wiring diagrams in good workshop manuals are illustrated with current flow charts, enabling faults to be traced by working in a methodical way, using the terminal numbers and the wiring colours.

Battery

Ex [4] Gd [3] Av [2] Po [1]

The battery is mounted in a prominent position in the front-right-corner of the engine compartment, when viewed from the front of the car. Check for corroded terminals and general condition. Beware, poor condition may suggest the vendor has charged the battery before you arrived!

The battery is located in the engine bay to the front-right of the car. The fluid bottles on this 16v Mk2 are radiator expansion tank (black cap), windscreen washer (cream cap) and steering fluid associated with optional power-steering (red cap below the battery).

Washer system

Ex [4] Gd [3] Av [2] Po [1]

Windscreen washers were factory fitted at the front and back on all models. The pipes are joined with rubber connectors and, as already mentioned, if the joint behind the side panel, forward of the right-hand rear light on the Mk2 becomes disconnected, a flooded boot will result. The washer bottle and pump motor are situated behind the battery on the Mk2 models and rarely cause trouble. The Mk1 is fitted with a separate rear washer system, with the bottle and pump situated in the right rear of the boot.

The Mk1 is fitted with a separate rear washer system, with the bottle and pump situated in the right rear of the boot.

Engine and transmission leaks

Ex [4] Gd [3] Av [2] Po [1]

Have a good look above and below the engine. Is it plastered with oil and muck? Remove the oil filler cap and check for mayonnaise-like gunge. These are both signs of a well-worn engine. Spilt oil at the top of the engine could be due to insufficient care being taken when topping up, or a perforated rocker cover, failed camshaft oil seal or leaky gasket. Looking lower down, the presence of oil at the cam-belt end of the engine, at the cylinder head to block joint, is usually attributable to the head-gasket failing. This can have serious implications for the alternator, as a good soaking with oil usually leads to failure. Gearbox oil has a very strong smell, so a leak here is easily detected.

Engine and transmission mountings

Ex [4] Gd [3] Av [2] Po [1]

The engine and gearbox are located in the chassis using three mounting points, one at the front of the engine and the other two on each side, towards the rear of the compartment. The front engine mount is due for replacement if you can easily lift the engine up and down by gripping the front mounting bracket.

Intake manifold and exhaust manifold

Ex [4] Gd [3] Av [2] Po [1]

The intake manifold holding the injectors gives very little trouble. The exhaust manifold, especially on the 16-valve model, can develop hairline cracks that eventually open-up and leak fumes. The 16-valve exhaust down-pipe to manifold flange is the work of the devil, requiring lots of patience when connecting or disconnecting.

Fuel injection system

Ex [4] Gd [3] Av [2] Po [1]

If the tick-over fluctuates between two distinct speeds, this could be due to a faulty idle stabilisation valve (below ignition leads), or the cold start valve (blue connector).

In 1988, the Digifant fuel injection unit, along with a new electronic ignition system, appeared on the eight-valve engine only.

If you're looking at a Mk1, inspect the condition of the fuel filler pipe. If it's rusty, or if the owner confirms that that it has been replaced recently, be cautious! If a rusty fuel filler has been replaced, ask if the tank was professionally flushed out at the same time – hopefully removing all traces of rusty particles. Providing the car is running OK you may be lucky! Otherwise it would become expensive in the near future if the rust particles migrate into the fuel injection unit.

The Bosch K-Jetronic fuel injection system is a relatively simple mechanical unit, with the fuel pressure maintained at a constant level by the pump mounted near the rear axle, on the right-hand side. The fuel is controlled by a large disc in the airflow meter, with the flow being dependant on the amount of air passing through the flap. The K-Jetronic system was used on all Mk1 GTIs, early Mk2 8-valve engines, and all 16-valve Mk2s until the end of production. The unit is fairly robust, its main enemy being the aforementioned rust particles. Fortunately, the rust issue doesn't apply to the Mk2, as plastic was used for both the tank and fuel filler neck. If the tick-over fluctuates between two distinct speeds, this could be due to a faulty idle stabilisation valve, or the cold start valve, or even the wrong value cold start valve being fitted. We know of a car where a cold start valve from an 8-valve was fitted as a temporary repair to a 16-valve engine, and the two speed tick-over wasn't cured until the correct unit was fitted.

In 1988, the Digifant fuel injection unit, along with a new electronic ignition system, appeared on the eight-valve engine.

Supercharger

Ex Gd Av Po
[4] [3] [2] [1]

If you are looking at a G60 or Rallye Golf, they have two important common factors: both were only available as left-hand-drive models, and each possessed a supercharger (known as a G-Lader due to the shape of the internals). These are notorious for losing power at around 40,000 to 50,000 miles, requiring at worst replacement, or at best refurbishment. You wouldn't want to know the price Volkswagen charges for a replacement, but there are companies out there that can refurbish a tired G-Lader for considerably less, providing the problems with the unit are detected early enough. They can also be rebuilt to give more power than the standard unit. Both the Rallye and G60 are the type of car that we would recommend you seek further advice about before parting with your hard earned cash.

If you are looking at a G60 or Rallye Golf, they have two important common factors: both were only available as left-hand-drive models, and each possessed a supercharger.

Examine the exhaust; it's a good bargaining point if not up to scratch.

Exhaust

Ex Gd Av Po
[4] [3] [2] [1]

Volkswagen would argue that the best and most efficient exhaust systems are the type fitted by the factory. However, a big proportion of the cars offered for sale will have an aftermarket exhaust at least from the down-pipe back, if not the whole system. These may vary from a cheap and cheerful system from the local tyre and exhaust centre, to a stainless steel masterpiece from a specialist in performance exhaust systems. While a tailpipe akin to a bucket may look the business, will you be able to stand the constant droning on a long trip down the motorway – the choice is yours! Carefully inspect the exhaust system for rusty endplates on the silencer boxes and leaking joints, also paying attention to the brackets and rubber mounting loops, as this could save you money – at least in the short term!

Gearbox, driveshafts (transmission) and clutch

Golf transmissions, four-speed until 1979 and five-speed thereafter, are relatively trouble-free, with only a few minor problems to look out for. Sometimes, you will find one that slips out of fifth gear. This can be diagnosed on a quiet road by accelerating and lifting off in quick succession to try and jolt it out of gear. The other fault is a tendency to crunch the gears between first and second due to worn synchromesh. While this is not too much of a problem in itself, small particles of metal can get knocked off the gears and cause wear throughout the transmission. Noisy transmissions are usually in the final drive (crown wheel and pinion). Wear problems here can be detected by alternating between first and reverse gears to see if there is any excessive slackness before the drive is taken up. The driveshafts can suffer from worn constant velocity joints, or split rubber gaiters. Visually check the constant velocity joint gaiters, for damage. Badly worn constant velocity joints click (mainly when cornering).

The Rallye Golf and the G60 have permanent all-wheel drive, so it would be advisable to enlist the services of an expert to inspect either of these versions. Parts and labour are likely to be prohibitively expensive if you make a hasty decision and end up with a lemon.

The clutch is checked for free-play at the pedal and should be between 10-20mm. Some models were fitted with an automatic adjusting clutch cable. Mk1 models have a weakness in the front bulkhead where the clutch cable passes through, leading to the outer cable pulling through and destroying the surrounding metal. You may find a welded-in repair panel, so this area is well worth checking for any weakness and the quality of any repair work found.

Examine the front bulkhead where the clutch cable passes through on Mk1 models. This has often been repaired with a welded in-panel.

Test drive (not less than 15 minutes)
Main warning lights (telltales)

After switching on the ignition, two instrument panel lights, the generator and oil pressure warning lights should go out when the engine is started. Later models have a warning buzzer in addition to a flashing oil pressure light. All models have a prominent warning light indicating when the handbrake is engaged. Lack of water in the cooling system will activate another important light.

Cold start

All GTIs have a cold start valve as part of the engine management within the fuel injection system. This rarely gives trouble, but alternating tick over speeds can indicate a problem with the valve.

Operation clutch

The clutch pedal, which should have 10-20mm of free-play before you can feel the spring pressure, can now be depressed and the gearlever should slip smoothly into first. On releasing the clutch it should not judder. A juddering clutch can be due to oil on the drive-plate, or simply mean that it is nearing the end of its life. On Mk1 models, any suspect feel to the clutch operation may be due to weak or corroded metal around the cable where it enters the bulkhead.

Operation gearbox (including reverse)

The gearbox fitted to a GTI will remain a very slick unit providing the vehicle has been maintained properly. Most problems arise from a worn linkage, or wear in the ball and cup at the base of the shift lever. When testing, drive the GTI fairly hard in each gear, making sure that it doesn't jump out of any them, especially fifth. Test reverse in this way, at somewhere quiet like an empty car park. Find reverse by pushing down on the lever, which is then moved to the left and forwards. Pay particular attention to the shift between first and second as this is where problems with the synchromesh are most likely to occur. This usually manifests itself as a crunching of the gears, which can lead to further problems if particles of gear teeth circulate in the transmission oil.

Steering feel

Although heavy against modern power-assisted vehicles, the steering should feel light and positive once on the move. The general tendency is towards under-steer, and the most stable technique is to approach a bend at a speed where you can gently accelerate through it. If you are too ambitious with your speed into a bend, lifting off will usually bring the car back into line. The Mk1 is more fun, as it feels more positive in a go-kart sort of way. (Note – power-steering was an optional extra on some later model Mk2s, while it became standard on all GTIs for the 1990 model year.)

Operation brakes (including handbrake)

The Mk1 GTI was often criticised for having brakes that were insufficient for the performance potential of the car. This was due to the remote servo on right-hand-drive cars being operated by a series of linkages across the car, leading to excessive pedal travel, rather than a fault with the actual brakes – in fact, the Mk1 brakes are satisfactory if correctly maintained. The Mk2 GTI overcame this by the servo being operated directly, and the addition of disc brakes on the rear. The disc brakes are relatively trouble-free unless a piston has seized in a calliper. The handbrake, if adjusted correctly to about four or five clicks, is a very capable devise that is able to hold the Golf on quite steep hills. If the handbrake on the Mk2 GTI feels dead when pulled up, and fails to hold the car on a hill, the mechanism on the rear callipers has probably seized – this is a fairly common problem. The drum brakes on the rear wheels of the Mk1 are fitted with a self-adjusting mechanism that, over time, can stick, causing longer pedal travel. This can usually be rectified during servicing by removing the burr on the outer edge of the drum and manually assisting the automatic mechanism to bring the shoes closer to the drum. A sticking wheel cylinder can cause uneven operation of the rear drum brakes, possibly resulting in the car pulling to one side during braking.

Noises

Ex 4   Gd 3   Av 2   Po 1

Hydraulic tappets can rattle for a while from start up. If the rattle persists they will need changing. A low rumble or whine from the back end can be due to a worn rear wheel bearing. A front wheel bearing can also whine but will be quieter during cornering when the bearing is under load. If the constant velocity joints on the double-jointed driveshafts 'click' when cornering, it's indicative of imminent failure. Transmission whine can be attributable to worn bearings or gears, while a clunk when taking up the drive can be due to wear in the CV cups. Mk1 dashboards are notorious for squeaks and rattles, while the heater fan on all models can be noisy if a leaf or similar piece of debris lurking in the fan housing moves into the blades.

Performance

Ex 4   Gd 3   Av 2   Po 1

See data chart, chapter 17 – pages 56-59.

Oil pressure

Ex 4   Gd 3   Av 2   Po 1

If the oil pressure warning light comes on when driving, especially if accompanied by a buzzer, stop immediately as this is an indication that there is hardly any oil pressure left. Check the oil level.

Charging rate

Ex 4   Gd 3   Av 2   Po 1

As long as the generator warning light stays off when driving, you can assume that it's charging OK. If the warning light comes on – stop immediately, as you could have a broken alternator belt. You may be able to get home if you don't meet any congestion, as the fan is operated by a thermostatic switch, but you will come to a halt eventually when you run out of battery power. The charging rate can be checked using a multi-meter, along with the techniques outlined in a good workshop manual.

Operation controls

Ex 4   Gd 3   Av 2   Po 1

All the major controls are similar to most vehicles of the era.

Operation switches

Ex 4   Gd 3   Av 2   Po 1

Rocker switches predominate, although slide controls operate the heater and ventilation system. The two steering column stalks are multi-functional, including the controls for the MFA computer, and are not quite as flimsy as their looks suggest. As with all plastic items, look out for damage caused by a combination of age and carelessness.

Ramp check

Ex 4   Gd 3   Av 2   Po 1

You may be able to persuade your local MOT or tyre depot to allow you to raise the GTI on their ramp, for a better visual inspection of the underside. Refer to previous evaluation chapters for the appropriate information and then pay particular attention to the following:

    If possible, have an assistant sitting in the Golf to press pedals and rock the steering. Inspect the flexible brake-pipes for cracking on the outer casing and check for bulging while your assistant presses the brake-pedal. Examine the metal brake-pipes for corrosion and signs of leaking. Have your assistant rock the steering when set straight-ahead, then in the right and left full-lock positions. While the steering is being rocked, check the steering track-rod ball-joints, steering-rack and steering-swivel ball-joints for excessive play. Inspect the under-body and chassis for corrosion, paying particular attention to the sills and jacking points. Look for signs of a leaky and corroded petrol filler pipe on a Mk1, it can cause considerable problems with the fuel injection system. Also on the Mk1, check the panel at the rear that joins the spare wheel well to the rear valence as this can suffer a build up of road dirt, leading to a bad dose of the tin worm. Check for engine and transmission oil-leaks. Pay attention to the driveshaft gaiters and the ball-joint covers. Inspect the condition of the exhaust system, paying particular attention to the ends of the silencers and the general condition of the catalytic converter if fitted. Check the condition of the exhaust heat shield.

A session on the ramp at a friendly garage will allow you a much better view of any chassis faults or fluid leakages. Mk1 Scirocco shown here.

Evaluation procedure

Add up the total points. Score: **176 = excellent, possibly concours; 132 = good; 88 = average; 44 = poor**. Cars scoring over 123 should be completely useable and require the minimum of repair, although continued maintenance and care will be required to keep them in condition. Cars scoring between 44-89 will require serious restoration (at much the same cost). Cars scoring between 90-122 will require very carefull assessment of necessary repair/restoration costs in order to reach a realistic value.

www.velocebooks.com / www.veloce.co.uk
All current books • New book news • Special offers • Gift vouchers

10 Auctions
– sold! Another way to buy your dream

Auction pros & cons
Pros: Prices will usually be lower than those of dealers or private sellers and you might grab a real bargain on the day. Auctioneers have usually established clear title with the seller. At the venue you can usually examine documentation relating to the vehicle.

Cons: You have to rely on a sketchy catalogue description of condition & history. The opportunity to inspect is limited and you cannot take the Golf on a performance test drive. Vehicles could well be a little below par and are likely to require some work. It's easy to overbid. There will usually be a buyer's premium to pay in addition to the auction hammer price.

Which auction?
Auctions by established auctioneers are advertised in car magazines and on the auction houses' websites. A catalogue, or a simple printed list of the lots for auctions might only be available a day or two ahead, though often lots are listed and pictured on auctioneers' websites much earlier. Contact the auction company to ask if previous auction selling prices are available as this is useful information (details of past sales are often available on websites).

Catalogue, entry fee and payment details
When you purchase the catalogue of the vehicles in the auction, it often acts as a ticket allowing two people to attend the viewing days and the auction. Catalogue details tend to be comparatively brief, but will include information such as 'one owner from new, low mileage, full service history', etc. It will also usually show a guide price to give you some idea of what to expect to pay and will tell you what is charged as a 'buyer's premium'. The catalogue will also contain details of acceptable forms of payment. At the fall of the hammer an immediate deposit is usually required, the balance payable within 24 hours. If the plan is to pay by cash there may be a cash limit. Some auctions will accept payment by debit card. Sometimes credit or charge cards are acceptable, but will often incur an extra charge. A bank draft or bank transfer will have to be arranged in advance with your own bank as well as with the auction house. No vehicle will be released before **all** payments are cleared. If delays occur in payment transfers then storage costs can accrue.

Buyer's premium
A buyer's premium will be added to the hammer price; **don't** forget this in your calculations. It is not usual for there to be a further state tax or local tax on the purchase price and/or on the buyer's premium.

Viewing
In some instances, it's possible to view on the day, or days before, as well as in the hours prior to the auction. There are auction officials available who are willing to help out by opening engine and luggage compartments and to allow you to inspect

the interior. While the officials may start the engine for you, a test drive is out of the question. Crawling under and around the Golf as much as you want is permitted, but you can't suggest that the vehicle you are interested in be jacked up, or attempt to do the job yourself. You can also ask to see any documentation available.

Bidding

Before you take part in the auction, **decide your maximum bid – and stick to it!**

It may take a while for the auctioneer to reach the lot you are interested in, so use that time to observe how other bidders behave. When it's the turn of your vehicle, attract the auctioneer's attention and make an early bid. The auctioneer will then look to you for a reaction every time another bid is made, usually the bids will be in fixed increments until the bidding slows, when smaller increments will often be accepted before the hammer falls. If you want to withdraw from the bidding, make sure the auctioneer understands your intentions – a vigorous shake of the head when he or she looks to you for the next bid should do the trick!

Assuming that you are the successful bidder the auctioneer will note your card or paddle number and, from that moment on, you will be responsible for the vehicle.

If the Golf is unsold, either because it failed to reach the reserve or because there was little interest, it may be possible to negotiate with the owner, via the auctioneers, after the sale is over.

Successful bid

There are two more items to think about; how to get the Golf home, and insurance. If you can't drive the vehicle, your own or a hired trailer is one way, another is to have the vehicle shipped using the facilities of a local company. The auction house will also have details of companies specialising in the transfer of all types of vehicle.

Insurance for immediate cover can usually be purchased on site, but it may be more cost-effective to make arrangements with your own insurance company in advance, and then call to confirm the full details. (Don't forget classic vehicle insurance where appropriate.)

eBay & other online auctions?

Buying this way could land you a GTI at a bargain price, though you'd be foolhardy to bid without examining the car first, something most vendors encourage. A useful feature of eBay is that the geographical location of the vehicle is shown, so you can narrow your choices to those within a realistic radius of home. Be prepared to be outbid in the last few moments of the auction. Remember, your bid is binding and that it will be very, very difficult to get restitution in the case of a crooked vendor fleecing you – caveat emptor!

Be aware that some vehicles offered for sale in online auctions are 'ghost' vehicles. **Don't** part with **any** cash without being sure that the Golf does actually exist and is as described (usually pre-bidding inspection is possible).

Auctioneers

Barrett-Jackson www.barrett-jackson.com, **Bonhams** www.bonhams.com, **British Car Auctions BCA** www.bca-europe.com or www.british-car-auctions.co.uk, **Cheffins** www.cheffins.co.uk, **Christies** www.christies.com, **Coys** www.coys.co.uk, **eBay** www.ebay.com, **H&H** www.classic-auctions.co.uk, **RM** www.rmauctions.com, **Shannons** www.shannons.com.au, **Silver** www.silverauctions.com

11 Paperwork
– correct documentation is essential!

The paper trail
The best Golfs come with a full service history, although other paperwork accumulated and passed on by as few previous owners as possible is valuable. This documentation represents the real history of the Golf, and from it can be deduced the level of care the vehicle has received, how much it's been used, which specialists have worked on it, and the dates of major repairs and restorations. All of this information will be priceless to you as the new owner, so be very wary of Golfs with little paperwork to support their claimed history.

Registration documents
All countries/states have some form of registration for private vehicles, whether it's like the American 'pink slip' system or the British 'log book' system.

It is essential to check that the registration document is genuine, that it relates to the Golf in question, and that all the vehicle's details are correctly recorded, including chassis/VIN and engine numbers (if these are shown). If you are buying from the previous owner, his or her name and address will be recorded in the document: this will not be the case if you are buying from a dealer.

In the UK, the current (Euro-aligned) registration document is named 'V5C', and is printed in coloured sections of blue, green and pink. The blue section relates to the vehicle's specification, the green section has details of the new owner, and the pink section is sent to the DVLA in the UK when the vehicle is sold. A small section in yellow deals with selling the car within the motor trade.

In the UK the DVLA will provide details of earlier keepers of the vehicle upon payment of a small fee, and much can be learned in this way.

If the Golf has a foreign registration there may be expensive and time-consuming formalities to complete. Do you really want the hassle?

Roadworthiness certificate
Most country/state administrations require that vehicles are regularly tested to prove that they are safe to use on the public highway and do not produce excessive emissions. In the UK that test (the 'MoT') is carried out at approved testing stations, for a fee. In the USA the requirement varies, but most states insist on an emissions test every two years as a minimum, while the police are charged with pulling over unsafe-looking vehicles.

In the UK, the test is required on an annual basis once a vehicle becomes three years old. Of particular relevance for older cars is that the certificate issued includes the mileage reading recorded at the test date and, therefore, becomes an independent record of that vehicle's history. Ask the seller if previous certificates are available. Without an MoT the vehicle should be hauled by trailer to its new home, unless you insist that a valid MoT is part of the deal (not such a bad idea this, as at least you will know the Golf was roadworthy on the day it was tested and you don't need to wait for the old certificate to expire before having the test done).

Road licence
The administration of every country/state charges some kind of tax for the use of its

road system, the actual form of the 'road licence', and how it is displayed, varying enormously country-to-country and state-to-state.

Whatever the form of the road licence, it must relate to the vehicle carrying it and must be present and valid if the vehicle is to be driven on the public highway legally. The value of the licence will depend on what duration it will be valid for.

In the UK, if a vehicle is untaxed because it has not been used for a period of time, the owner has to inform the licensing authorities; otherwise the vehicle's date-related registration number will be lost and there will be a painful amount of paperwork to get it re-registered.

Valuation certificate

It is possible, but in the case of the relatively low value Golf not probable, that a vendor will have a recent valuation certificate or letter signed by a recognised expert, stating how much he or she believes the particular Golf to be worth (such documents, together with photos, are usually needed to get 'agreed value' insurance). Generally, such documents should act only as confirmation of your own assessment of the Golf, rather than a guarantee of value, as the expert might not have seen the vehicle in the metal. The easiest way to find out how to obtain a formal valuation is to contact the owners' club.

Service history

Most Mk1 and 2 Golfs are most likely to have been serviced at home by enthusiastic (and hopefully capable) owners for a good number of years. Nevertheless, try to obtain as much service history and other paperwork pertaining to the Golf as you can. Naturally, dealer stamps or specialist garage receipts score most points in the value stakes. However, anything helps in the great authenticity game, items like the original bill of sale, handbook, parts invoices and repair bills, adding to the story and the character of the Golf. In the relatively unlikely event of the seller claiming that the Golf has been restored, then expect receipts where professional work has been carried out, and other evidence, particularly photographic, where the work has been done at home.

If the seller claims to have carried out regular servicing, ask when and what work was completed, and seek some evidence of it being carried out. Your assessment of the Golfs overall condition should tell you whether the seller's claims are genuine.

12 What's it worth to you?
– let your head rule your heart!

Condition

If the Golf you've been looking at is really bad then you've probably, wisely, not bothered to use the marking system in chapter 9-60 minute evaluation. Walk away unless the car is a Rallye Golf and, even then, only continue with extreme caution.

If you did use the marking system in chapter 9 you'll know whether the Golf is in Excellent (maybe Concours), Good, Average or Poor condition or, perhaps, somewhere in-between these categories.

As yet most Golf GTIs and associated models don't fetch particularly high prices. Mk2 models are still commonplace. Checkout the prices asked in the specialist VW magazines, but bear in mind that the seller is likely to be an enthusiast selling to another enthusiast. Concours winners and special edition models are likely to command the highest of prices. With regard to customised and beefy examples, there is no set rule – you must only pay what you consider to be a fair price.

If you are buying from a dealer, remember there will be a dealer's premium on the price.

Striking a deal

Negotiate on the basis of your condition assessment, and fault rectification cost. Also take into account the Golf's specification. Be realistic about the value, but don't be completely intractable: a small compromise on the part of the vendor or buyer will often facilitate a deal at little real cost.

13 Do you really want to restore?
– it'll take longer and cost more than you think

The biggest cost involved in any restoration project put into the hands of professionals is not the parts you'll need, or the materials involved, but labour. Such restorations don't come cheap, and as yet, GTIs other than very early examples have not become so scarce that a un-restored, decent example can't be found elsewhere. However, if you are determined to go ahead there are three other issues to consider when dealing with the trade.

Would you want to restore this Golf? If it was one of the earliest GTIs from late 1976, yes; otherwise no, there are still plenty to choose from.

With this amount of impact damage, restoration would probably only be considered if the model was particularly rare.

First, make it abundantly clear what you want doing. It's no use simply indicating that the GTI needs to be restored. For example, are all replacement panels to be new old stock (NOS), or at least correct for the year? Is a re-spray to be a bare metal one? Should all window glass be removed prior to painting? The list is endless if you are going to be fair to the professionals, and in turn they are to give you the result required.

Secondly, make sure that not only is a detailed estimate involved, but also that it is more or less binding. There are too many stories of a person quoted one figure only to be presented with an invoice for a far greater one!

Thirdly, check that the company you are dealing with has a good reputation. There have been examples reported of quite well known names whose work has, in years gone by, shown to be disappointing at best. You don't want to be faced with the prospect of having a GTI restored for a second time.

Restoring a Golf GTI yourself requires a number of skills, which if you already have them is marvellous, but acquiring the same might not be an overnight process. Can you weld, can you prepare and spray a vehicle yourself, can you rebuild an engine and have you got the equipment? Of course you might select to oversee a project, but have you sufficient friends with the expertise to accomplish all you require? Above all, have your contacts got time to do the jobs you want according to the schedule you set?

This immaculate Mk1 Campaign special edition has had considerable time and money lavished on it in order to maintain this condition.

Be prepared for a top-notch professional to put you on a lengthy waiting list or, if tackling a restoration yourself, expect things to go wrong and set aside extra time to complete the task.

14 Paint problems
– a bad complexion, including dimples, pimples and bubbles

Paint faults generally occur due to lack of protection/maintenance, or to poor preparation prior to a respray or touch-up. Some of the following conditions may be present in the car you're looking at:

Orange peel
This appears as an uneven paint surface, similar to the appearance of the skin of an orange. The fault is caused by the failure of atomised paint droplets to flow into each other when they hit the surface. It's sometimes possible to rub out the effect with proprietary paint cutting/rubbing compound or very fine grades of abrasive paper. A respray may be necessary in severe cases. Consult a bodywork repairer/paint shop for advice on the particular vehicle.

Cracking
Severe cases are likely to have been caused by too heavy an application of paint (or filler beneath the paint). Also, insufficient stirring of the paint before application can lead to the components being improperly mixed, and cracking can result. Incompatibility with the paint already on the panel can have a similar effect. To rectify, it is necessary to rub down to a smooth, sound finish before re-spraying the problem area.

Cracking, due here to the filler beneath the paint lifting.

Crazing
Sometimes the paint takes on a crazed, rather than a cracked, appearance when the problems mentioned under 'Cracking' are present. This problem can also be caused by a reaction between the underlying surface and the paint. Paint removal and re-spraying the problem area is usually the only solution.

Blistering
Almost always caused by corrosion of the metal beneath the paint. Usually perforation will be found in the metal and the damage will usually be worse than that suggested by the area of blistering. The metal will have to be repaired before repainting.

Blistering is usually caused by corroded metal beneath the paint surface. The metal is usually perforated with the damage more extensive than the blister would suggest. The affected metal will need replacing before the area is repainted.

Micro blistering
Usually the result of an economy re-spray where inadequate heating has allowed moisture to settle on the vehicle before spraying. Consult a paint specialist, but usually damaged paint will have to be removed before partial or full re-spraying. Can also be caused by vehicle covers that don't 'breathe.'

Micro blistering.

Fading

Some colours, especially reds, are prone to fading if subjected to strong sunlight for long periods without the benefit of polish protection. Sometimes proprietary paint restorers and/or paint cutting/rubbing compounds will retrieve the situation. Often a re-spray is the only real solution.

This repair has faded because the metallic paint was not protected by clear lacquer.

Faded paint can sometimes be remedied with a good dose of T-cut.

Peeling

Often a problem with metallic paintwork when the sealing lacquer becomes damaged and begins to peel off. Poorly applied paint may also peel. The remedy is to strip and start again!

The lacquer is peeling, causing problems with the metallic paint beneath.

Dimples

Dimples in the paintwork are caused by the residue of polish (particularly silicone types) not being removed properly before re-spraying. Paint removal and repainting is the only solution.

Dents

Small dents are usually easily cured by the 'Dentmaster', or equivalent process, that sucks or pushes out the dent (as long as the paint surface is still intact). Companies offering dent removal services usually come to your home: consult your telephone directory.

15 Problems due to lack of use
– just like their owners, Golf GTIs need exercise!

Golf GTIs, like humans, are at their most efficient if they exercise regularly. A run of at least 10 miles, once a week is recommended, except when salt is spread on the road.

Seized components

Pistons in brake callipers, slave and master cylinders can seize. The clutch may seize if the plate becomes stuck to the flywheel because of corrosion. Handbrakes (parking brakes) can seize if the cables and linkages rust. This can be a problem with the handbrake mechanism of the rear callipers fitted to the Mk2 GTI. Pistons can seize in the bores due to corrosion. Brakes can bind due to corrosion on discs and drums.

Rust can form on the brake discs or drums, eventually causing them to seize solid.

Fluids

Old, acidic oil can corrode bearings. Check the oil on the dipstick. If the engine has not run for some time, it's likely that the carbon and sludge that was suspended in the oil, has now settled out as a black acidic deposit on all the internal surfaces. This can usually be sorted with an oil change, followed by another after 500 gently driven miles. In a worst-case scenario, the acid in the oil could have attacked the crankshaft and other engine bearings, resulting in trouble further down the line.

Uninhibited coolant can corrode internal waterways. Lack of antifreeze can cause core plugs to be pushed out, even cracks in the block or head. Silt in the cooling system settling and solidifying can cause overheating.

Most types of brake fluid are hydroscopic, absorbing water from the atmosphere, and should be renewed every two years. Old brake fluid containing high water content can cause corrosion, leading to the pistons in callipers, master cylinder and slave cylinders to seize (freeze). The water content could lead to catastrophic brake failure when the water turns to vapour within the hot braking system.

Tyre problems

Tyres that have had the weight of the car on them in a single position for some time will develop flat spots, resulting in some (usually temporary) vibration. The tyre walls may have cracks or (blister-type) bulges, not ideal in a high performance car like a Golf GTI. In the interest of safety we would recommend new tyres if any of the above faults became evident.

If a car has been standing for a long time, the tyres will develop flat spots. For the sake of safety, change them at the earliest opportunity.

Shock absorbers (dampers)

The seals within the dampers can break down due to lack of use, resulting in fluid loss. Visually check each shock absorber for fluid loss and then press down on each corner to check efficiency. After pressing down, the car should return to normal ride height without bouncing further. Evidence of either fault would result in an MoT failure.

A lot of GTIs have been fitted with adjustable sports suspension kits which often use stiffer gas filled dampers and shorter springs to achieve a lower stance. These kits are often adjustable to achieve the desired ride height. The adjusting mechanism could corrode and seize up after a prolonged period of inactivity.

Rubber and plastic

Window and door seals can harden and leak. Gaiters/boots can crack. Wiper blades will harden. The black plastic bumpers, wheelarch trims and side rubbing strips can fade badly, but are usually restorable with proprietary bumper and trim restoring fluid or a careful application of heat from a hot air paint stripper.

The rear window rubber has cracked and the vinyl trim is lifting, causing the owner to apply tape as a temporary repair.

Electrics

The battery will be of little use if it has not been charged for many months. Earthing/grounding problems are common when the connections have corroded. Fuses may rust/corrode and will need cleaning up with fine-grain emery paper and spraying with electrical cleaning fluid.

Most circuits use either 6.3mm spade connectors or multi-plugs, which can be restored using electrical contact cleaning fluid to maintain peak efficiency and avoid voltage drops. Sparkplug electrodes will often have corroded in an unused engine. Wiring insulation can harden and fail.

Rotting exhaust system

Exhaust gas contains a high water content, so exhaust systems corrode very quickly from the inside when a vehicle is not used. Expect to replace the exhaust system on any GTI that has stood idle for 6-months or more. The rubber exhaust support loops also seem to perish quicker on an unused vehicle.

16 The Community
– key people, organisations and companies in the GTI world

Auctioneers
Barrett-Jackson
www.barrett-jackson.com

Bonhams
www.bonhams.com

British Car Auctions (BCA)
www.bca-europe.com
www.british-car-auctions.co.uk

Cheffins
www.cheffins.co.uk

Christies
www.christies.com

Coys
www.coys.co.uk

eBay
www.ebay.com

H&H
www.classic-auctions.co.uk

RM
www.rmauctions.com

Shannons
www.shannons.com.au

Silver
www.silverauctions.com

Clubs across the world
Australia
Club Vee Dub Sydney
www.clubvw.org.au

Volkswagen Club Victoria
www.vwclub.com.au

Germany
All-VW-Club Neiderflur
www.neiderflur.de

South Africa
VW Club of South Africa
www.vwclub.co.za

UK
Club GTI
www.clubgti.com

Cornwall Volkswagen Owners Club
Cornwall, U.K.
www.cvwoc.co.uk

Mk1 Golf Owners Club
www.vwgolfmk1.org.uk

Mk2 Golf Owners Club
www.vwgolfmk2.co.uk

Volkswagen Owners Club
c/o PO Box 7, Burntwood, Staffs. WS7
2SB. Tel 01952 242167
www.vwocgb.com
The oldest VW club in Britain. Caters
for all models whether water-cooled or
air-cooled.

USA
For a list of clubs visit:
www.hubcapcafe.com/resources/
volkswagen_clubs.htm

Specialists
There are so many businesses
specialising in Golf performance tuning
and sales that we have restricted our
listing to UK names. This list does
not imply recommendation and is not
deemed to be comprehensive.

AmD Technik (High performance Tuning)
Woking, Surrey. Tel 01932 703568
West Thurrock, Essex.
Tel 01708 861827
www.amdtechnik.com

C&R Enterprises (performance tuning
and servicing)
Nottingham. Tel 01159 785740
www.candrenterprises.co.uk

Euro Car Parts (Parts supplier)
Branches nationwide.
Tel 0870 150 6506
www.eurocarparts.com

German Swedish & French (Parts)
Branches all over the country.
Mail order tel 020 8917 3866
www.gsfcarparts.com

Jabbasport (specialists in forced
induction tuning)
Also supercharger rebuilds and
gearboxes.
Crowland, Peterborough.
Tel 01733 211779
www.jabbasport.com

Richard Hulin (Repairs and Spares)
Tel 01452 502333 (Gloucester)

Stevens VW Dismantlers (VW salvage)
Chelmsford, Essex
Tel 01245 362020
www.vws.me.uk

Volks-Apart (VW Salvage)
Tel 020 8309 6200
www.volkswagenspares.com
Volksgoods (Electrical parts)
Tel 01522 751941

Volkswizard
Sales of used Golf GTI and other water-
cooled models.
www.volkswizard.co.uk

WagonWheels
Sales, parts and servicing of early GTI
models
Copythorne, Southampton
Tel 07946 503450
www.wagonwheels.co.uk

Books
Sadly not many books remain in print
– to the best of our knowledge the
following are still available.

You and Your Volkswagen Golf GTI
Andy Butler, *Haynes* 2001

VW Golf Laurence Meredith, *Sutton
Publishing* 1999

***VW Golf: Five Generations of
Fun*** Richard Copping, photos Ken
Cservenka, Veloce 2006

***VW Golf GTI Limited Edition Extra
1976-1991*** Brooklands Books

17 Vital statistics
– essential data at your fingertips

Number built – between 1976, the first year of GTI production, and 1991, the last full year of the Mk2, annual numbers for all Golfs varied from 527,000 to 908,000. As an example of the role the GTI played in such numbers, in 1983 71,000 such cars were sold in mainland Europe, with 6148 sales being made in the UK.

Mk1 GTI 1600 1976
Engine
Transversely mounted four cylinder in-line

Capacity	1588cc
Bore and stroke	79.5mm x 80mm
Compression ratio	9.5:1
Fuel injection	Bosch K-Jetronic
Max. power	110bhp at 6100rpm
Max. torque	103lb.ft at 5000rpm

Performance
Top speed	110mph
0-50mph	6.1sec
0-62mph	9.0sec

Transmission
Gearbox	4-speed manual
Ratios 1st	3.45
2nd	1.94
3rd	1.37
4th	0.97
Final drive	3.70 to 1

Suspension and steering
Front	MacPherson struts, coil springs, anti-roll bar
Rear	Torsion beam, trailing arms, coil springs, anti-roll bar

Suspension lowered by 15mm compared to other Mk1 Golfs

Steering	Maintenance-free self-adjusting rack and pinion
Tyres	175/70 HR 13
Wheels	5.5Jx13 (Initially 12-spoke alloys – then steel for UK market until 1980)

Brakes
Type	Diagonally divided dual circuit with brake servo and brake pressure regulator
Size	Front 9.4in diameter discs, internally ventilated. Rear 7.1in diameter self-adjusting drums

Dimensions
Track	Front 1404mm (55.3in)
	Rear 1372mm (54.0in)
Wheelbase	2400mm (94.5in)
Overall length	3705mm (145.9in)
Overall width	1628mm (64.1in)
Overall height	1390mm (54.7in)
Unladen weight	810kg (1786lb)

Golf GTI MK1 1800, 1983 (Only differences to 1600 at launch listed)
Engine
Capacity	1781cc
Bore and stroke	81mm x 86.4mm
Compression ratio	10:1
Max. power	112bhp at 5800rpm
Max. torque	109lb.ft at 3500rpm

Performance
Top speed	114mph
0-50mph	6.2sec
0-62mph	8.2sec

Transmission
Gearbox	5-speed all indirect with synchromesh
Clutch	Single dry plate
Ratios 1st	3.45
2nd	2.12

3rd	1.44
4th	1.13
5th	0.91
Final drive	3.65 to 1

Suspension and steering
Wheels	5.5Jx13 alloys

Dimensions
Overall length	3815mm (150.2in)
Overall height	1395mm (54.9in)
Unladen weight	860kg (1896lb)

(Quoted by Volkswagen for both the
three- and five-door model!)

Golf GTI MK2 8-valve 1984

Engine
Transversely mounted four cylinder
in-line

Capacity	1781cc
Bore and stroke	81mm x 86.4mm
Compression ratio	10:1
Fuel injection	Bosch K-Jetronic Digifant from 1988 on 8v only. 16v retained K-Jetronic throughout.
Max. power	112bhp at 5500rpm
Max. torque	115lb.ft at 3100rpm

Performance
Top speed	119mph
0-50mph	6.5sec
0-62mph	8.3sec

Transmission
Gearbox		5-speed all indirect with synchromesh
Clutch		Single dry plate
Ratios	1st	3.46
	2nd	2.12
	3rd	1.44
	4th	1.13
	5th	0.89
Final drive		3.67 to 1

Suspension and steering
Front	MacPherson strut and lower wishbone, 18mm anti-roll bar
Rear	Torsion beam, trailing arms, 20mm anti-roll bar
Steering	Maintenance-free self-adjusting rack and pinion
Tyres	185/60 HR 14
Wheels	6Jx14 – alloys standard on five-door – optional on three door

Brakes
Type	Diagonally divided dual circuit with brake servo and brake pressure regulator
Size	Front 239mm (9.4in) diameter discs, internally ventilated – single piston sliding calliper Rear 226mm (8.9in) solid disc and single piston sliding calliper

Dimensions
Track	Front 1427mm (56.2in) Rear 1422mm (56in)
Wheelbase	2475mm (97.4in)
Overall length	3985mm (156.9in)
Overall width	1680mm (66.1in)
Overall height	1405mm (55.3in)
Unladen weight	920kg (2029lb) 3-door, 940 kg (2072lb) 5-door

Golf GTI MK2 16-valve 1986 (Only differences to 8-valve at launch listed)

Engine
Belt and chain driven twin-overhead
camshaft with two inlet and two exhaust
valves per cylinder

Max. power	139bhp at 6100rpm
Max. torque	123.5lb.ft at 4600rpm

Performance

Top speed	129mph
0-50mph	6.0sec
0-62mph	7.9 sec

Suspension and steering

Tyres	185/60 VR 14
Wheels	6Jx14 alloys standard

Dimensions

Unladen weight	960kg (2117lb)
	VW official figures

The Rallye Golf 1989

Engine

Transversely mounted four cylinder in-line. Five bearing crankshaft. Valve control through toothed belt driven, single overhead camshaft. Mechanical supercharger (G60-charger) with charge pressure control. Intercooler operated by air flow. G60 supercharger runs at 1.7 times engine speed, delivering 0.65 bar (9.4psi) maximum boost

Bore and stroke	80.6mm x 86.4mm
Capacity	1763cc
Compression ratio	8:1
Fuel injection	Digifant
Max. power	160bhp at 5600rpm
Max. torque	166lb.ft at 4000rpm
Fuel capacity	55 litres (12.1 imp gallons) but different location compared to other models

Performance

Top speed	130mph
0-50mph	5.6sec
0-62mph	8.6sec

Transmission

Permanent four-wheel-drive with slip-dependent power distribution to front and rear wheels. Drive to front wheels via differential and half shafts with constant velocity joints. Drive to rear wheels via bevel gears, three-piece propeller shaft and viscous coupling. Final drive with freewheel integrated between bevel gears and differential.

Gearbox		5-speed manual
Clutch		Single dry plate
Ratios	1st	3.78
	2nd	2.11
	3rd	1.34
	4th	0.97
	5th	0.80
Final drive		3.68 to 1

Suspension and steering

Front	MacPherson struts and lower wishbones, coil springs 23mm anti-roll bar
Rear	Semi-trailing wishbones, coil spring struts, 21mm anti-roll bar

Lowered by 20mm compared to ordinary models

Steering	Maintenance-free power-steering self-adjusting rack and pinion
Tyres	205/50 15 VR
Wheels	6Jx15 Sebring alloys

Brakes

Type	Diagonally divided dual circuit with brake servo and load sensitive brake pressure regulator. Electronic Teves anti-lock brake system (ABS)
Size	Front – 280mm (11.0in) diameter discs, internally ventilated Rear – solid disc from the Polo front fitted with Golf callipers

Dimensions

Track	Front 1429mm (56.3in)
	Rear 1434mm (56.5in)
Wheelbase	2479mm (97.6in)
Overall length	4035mm (158.9in)
Overall width	1700mm (66.9in)
Overall height	1399mm (55.1in)
Unladen weight	1195Kg (2635lb)

Mk2 GTI G60 1990 (only differences to Rallye Golf listed)

Engine

Bore and stroke	81.0mm x 86.4mm
Capacity	1781cc
Max. power	160bhp at 5800rpm
Max. torque	166lb.ft at 3800rpm
Fuel capacity	55 litres (12.1 imp gallons) in normal Golf location

Performance

Top speed	134mph
0-50mph	5.7sec
0-62mph	8.3sec

Transmission

Ratios	1st	3.78
	2nd	2.12
	3rd	1.34
	4th	0.97
	5th	0.76
Final drive		3.67 to 1

Suspension and steering

Rear	Semi-trailing wishbones, coil spring struts, 21mm anti-roll bar

Lowered by 20mm at the front and 10mm at the rear compared to ordinary models

Tyres	185/55 R 15V, or 195/50 R 15V
Wheels	6Jx15 steel, or 6.5Jx15 BBS alloys

Brakes/traction

EDL (Electronic Differential Lock) optional

Dimensions

Track	Front 1433mm (56.4in)
	Rear 1428mm (56.2in)
Wheelbase	2475mm (97.4in)
Overall length	4040mm (159in)
Overall width	1700mm (66.9in)
Overall height	1400mm (55.1in)
Unladen weight	1080Kg (2381lb) 2-door 1105kg (2436lb) 4-door

The Essential Buyer's Guide™

The Essential Buyer's Guide
ALFA ROMEO GIULIA
GT COUPÉ
978-1-904788-69-0

The Essential Buyer's Guide
ALFA ROMEO GIULIA
SPIDER
978-1-904788-98-0

The Essential Buyer's Guide
BMW
GS
978-1-84584-135-5

The Essential Buyer's Guide
BSA
500 & 650 Twins
A7, A10, A50 & A65 1946 to 1973
978-1-84584-136-2

The Essential Buyer's Guide
CITROËN
2CV
978-1-845840-99-0

The Essential Buyer's Guide
PORSCHE
928
978-1-904788-70-6

The Essential Buyer's Guide
MERCEDES-BENZ
280-560SL & SLC
W107 series Roadsters & Coupés 1971 to 1989
978-1-845841-07-2

The Essential Buyer's Guide
MG
MGB
MGB GT
978-1-845840-29-7

The Essential Buyer's Guide
MORRIS
MINOR & 1000
Saloons, Travellers & Convertibles 1952 to 1971
978-1-845841-01-0

The Essential Buyer's Guide
SUBARU
IMPREZA
All turbo models 1992 to 2007
978-1-845841-63-8

The Essential Buyer's Guide
ROLLS-ROYCE
SILVER SHADOW
BENTLEY
T-SERIES
Including Corniche, Camargue, Silver Shadow II & Bentley T2, 1965 to 1980
978-1-84584-146-1

The Essential Buyer's Guide
BSA
Bantam
All models 1948 to 1971
978-1-84584-165-2

The Essential Buyer's Guide
JAGUAR
E-type
V12 5.3 litre
978-1845840-77-8

The Essential Buyer's Guide
JAGUAR
E-type
3.8 & 4.2 litre
978-1-904788-85-0

The Essential Buyer's Guide
CITROËN
DS & ID
All models 1966 to 1975
978-1-84584-138-6

The Essential Buyer's Guide
JAGUAR/DAIMLER
XJ6, XJ12
& Sovereign
All Jaguar/Daimler/VDP series I, II & III models 1968 to 1992
978-1-845841-19-5

The Essential Buyer's Guide
MERCEDES-BENZ PAGODA
230, 250 & 280SL
W113 series Roadsters & Coupés 1963 to 1971
978-1-845841-13-3

The Essential Buyer's Guide
MINI
All Mk1 editions, saloon, vans and pick-ups 1959-1969
978-1-84584-204-8

The Essential Buyer's Guide
FIAT
500 & 600
1955 to 1992
Saloons/Sedans, Multipla, Giardinera & 126
978-1-84584-147-8

The Essential Buyer's Guide
TRIUMPH
BONNEVILLE
978-1-84584-134-8

The Essential Buyer's Guide
Triumph
TR6
978-1-845840-26-6

The Essential Buyer's Guide
VOLKSWAGEN
BEETLE
978-1-904788-72-0

The Essential Buyer's Guide
VOLKSWAGEN
BUS
978-1-845840-22-8

The Essential Buyer's Guide
Jaguar/Daimler
XJ
An all 6, 4.2 & 12 cylinder models, XJ40, 1994 to 2003
978-1-84584-200-0

The Essential Buyer's Guide
Jaguar/Daimler
XJ40
All models 1986 to 1994
978-1-84584-192-8

The Essential Buyer's Guide
JAGUAR
XJ-S
All 6 and 12 cylinder models 1975 to 1996
978-1-84584-161-4

£9.99*/$19.95*

*prices subject to change • p&p extra • for more
details visit www.veloce.co.uk or
email info@veloce.co.uk

Also from Veloce ...

*£19.99 paperback
176 pages
Over 650 black and white photographs
ISBN: 978-1-903706-93-0

A comprehensive guide to all the Volkswagens not built in Germany, and the unusual ones that were. Includes VW type designations, chassis numbers, VW options, buggies, military, police, utility vehicles and all the lesser known models produced by VW around the world.

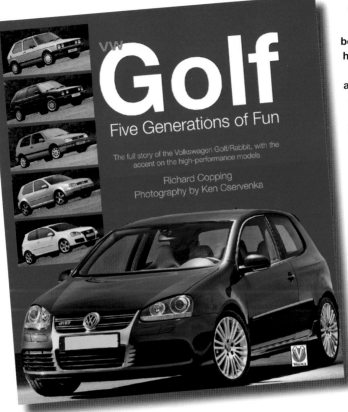

Index